AF653903

TRADITIONAL ADMINISTRATIVE SYSTEM AND CUSTOMARY LAWS OF THE THANGKHALS

The Author

Dr. S. Haukhanlian Mate (b.1972) Ph.D. from Manipur University, joined various academic associations. He is a life member of Mizo History Association, North East India History Association, Indian History Congress and Mizoram Academic Forum. He has presented a number of research papers at International, National and State Level Seminars.

Presently he is working as Associate Professor in the Deptt. of History at Government Saitual College (Mizoram). He also works as the Programme Officer of the National Service Scheme (NSS) Unit of the College.

Traditional Administrative System and Customary Laws of the Thangkhals

S. HAUKHANLIAN MATE

Akansha Publishing House
Delhi • Guwahati • Visakhapatnam

AKANSHA PUBLISHING HOUSE
4649/21-B, Ansari Road
Daryaganj, New Delhi - 110 002
Phones: 23263193, 9435116718
Email: ektabooks@yahoo.com
Visit us: www.akanshapublishinghousc.com

Traditional Administrative System and Customary Laws of the Thangkhals

© Author

First Published, 2014

ISBN 978-81-8370-400-7

[No part of this publication may be reproduced, stored in a retrieval system or transmitted, in any form or by any means, mechanical, photocopying, recording or otherwise, without prior written permission of the author/publisher].

PRINTED IN INDIA

Published by Akansha Publishing House, New Delhi - 110 002 and Printed at Harmain Offset Press, Delhi.

In Memory of
My Beloved Late parents
S. KAMCHINHANG MATE (1933-2007)
and
CHINGZANIAN (1936-2011)
who were very dear to me.

Contents

Preface

Until now, the Thangkhals who belongs to the Chin-Kuki-Mizo ethnic group had not received any (adequate) attention at the hands of the historians. There is no book written on the tribe with proper research work. In recent years, some research works are done on the tribe like "The Study of the Thangkhal Tribe in Manipur", by Niangdeihnuam in her M. Phil. Dissertation in 2008 and "A study of Christianity among the Thangkhals" by T. Chinminlian in his B.Th. Dissertation in 2011. But these two works did not give a detailed account of the administrative system and customary laws of the tribe.

The present work, "Traditional Administrative System and Customary Laws of the Thangkhals" aims at a comprehensive study of the Thangkhal Traditional Administrative System and their Customary Laws. The study is divided into five chapters. Chapter I deal with the introduction of the research work, objectives, hypothesis, Literature on the tribe and related tribes, methodology employed, significance of the work and the limitation of the study. The second chapter deals with the origin and migratory routes of the tribe. It also discusses their early and present settlements. The third chapter deals with the Traditional Administrative System of the Thangkhals. It discussed the power and privileges enjoyed by important functionaries like Hausa (Chief), Manchili (Deputy Chief), Siampu (priest), Sikkheng (blacksmith), Tangsaam (crier) and Val-Upa (youth commander). The fourth chapter gives a comprehensive study of the Customary Laws and practices of the Thangkhals. Customary laws dealing with marriage, divorce, widow remarriage, inheritance, fines and punishments, etc. are elaborately discussed in this chapter. The fifth chapter contains the conclusions. It is an overall summing up of all the findings of the previous chapters.

The present work is an outcome of my University Grants Commission Minor Research Project, "Traditional Administrative System and Customary Laws of the Thangkhals of Manipur", submitted to University Grants Commission (UGC), North Eastern Regional Office (NERO), Guwahati in November, 2012. Here it has been slightly modified without making any substantial change.

In connection with this work, I am deeply indebted to the UGC, NERO, Guwahati for accepting my proposal on the Minor Research Project, "Traditional Administrative System and Customary laws of the Thangkhals of Manipur", and financially sanctioning the Research Project for its timely completion. Without the financial support of UGC (NERO), the Research Project work would not have been materialized.

I am greatly indebted to those persons whom I always disturbed during the course of my research work. Out of the many, mention may be made of Mr. S. Kampau Mate, my elder brother who always help me and encouraged me during the course of the work and Mr. Kamlianthang, my nephew who accompanied me in my field works. I do acknowledge my debt of gratitude to those elders whom I interviewed during my field works. I really extended my thanks for their kind help and cooperation. I also take this opportunity to express my gratitude to my Principal, Dr. Lalsiamhnuna for his official approval and permission and also encouragement to undertake and complete the research work.

I am also greatly indebted to Prof. Lal Dena, a retired professor from Manipur University for going through the manuscripts.

I am also deeply grateful to my wife, Ms. Ruthi Lalrempuii who always encouraged and helped me throughout the course of the research work and look after the home front so that I could give more attention to my work.

I do convey my cordial thanks to my publisher, Akansha Publishing House, New Delhi for having taken utmost care and responsibility to publish this book in such a short time.

Above all, I give my thanks to the Almighty God for His blessing, Divine love and guidance which enabled me to complete this work.

S. Haukhanlian Mate

CHAPTER 1

Introduction

The Thangkhals belongs to the Mongoloid stock of the Kuki-Chin-Mizo group of tribes presently spreading across the Indo-Burma border and as far as the Chittagong Hill Tract in Bangladesh. They claimed their origin from 'Khul' which means cave, a place which has not been ascertained to any degree of certainty as their traditional home. According to their verbal tradition, the Thangkhals came out of Khul under the leadership of Pu Zahong and also settled at a place called Ciimnuai (Chhimnuai). Here all the cognate tribes of Kuki-Chin-Mizo are said to have lived together peacefully for a long time.

The Thangkhals belongs to Tibeto-Burman family speaking the Tibeto-Burman language. The original home of these people is not definitely known but must be somewhere between Kansu in South China and Burma is believed to be their earliest known home. According to Hall, the earliest known home of the Tibeto-Burmese speaking people was somewhere between Gopi desert and Northeast of Tibet also possible Kansu. This region forms parts of Southern China where the tribal people are found and distributed widely over the mountainous area of Kweichow,

Szechwan and Yunnan. The Thangkhals, who were also a tribal people were believed to have lived with other tribes in these areas. Thus, the southern China between Kansu and Burma may be considered as the original homes of the tribal peoples including the Thangkhals. From southern China, the people with other tribal groups started their sojourn and some had gone to Tibet, some to Nepal and some moved towards Burma and lived there. As there was peace in Burma, they started moving in different directions and the Thangkhal group moves towards the south and lived mostly with what we called now as the Sukte tribes. Till now, no tribal group has their own identity as it is now.

The first known settlement of the Thangkhals in the Chin Hills was Ciimnuai (Chhimnuai). From this place, they founded a new village called Taitaam. After living for several years in this village, they moved to a village called Mualbem. It is believed that till now the Thangkhals lived together with their cognate tribes of Kuki-Chin-Mizo groups. From Mualbem village, a group of people moved out and founded a new village known as the Thangkhal village. In course of time, the people who lived in this village developed a distinct culture, tradition and dialect which are quite distinct from other tribes of the Kuki-Chin-Mizo groups. As such, taking the name of the village, the people called themselves "Thangkhal'. Thus, the Thangkhal tribe came into existence who have distinct custom, tradition and dialect and customary laws which are quite different from that of their cognate tribes.

From the Thangkhal village which is in the Chin Hills of Burma, the people moved to Manipur. In the Administrative Report for 1877-78, a remarkable circumstance in connection with the Sootie (Sukte) tribe and Manipur is recorded. Parties to the number of over 2,000 persons belonging to the Sooties migrated during the year into Manipur territory, where they settled down on land assigned to them by the Maharajah in the neighborhood of Moirang, to the south-west of the valley. The Political Agent was visited by the chiefs of the immigrants, who expect the number to be increased that year. Colonel Johnstone considered the immigrant important. The Sooties weakened by the loss of 2000 of their number and with the early prospect of losing more, will be less formidable to Manipur. The new comers are mostly not actually of the Sootie tribe but are reported to belong to a Helot race living in villages of their own among the Sooties. Their object in leaving their country was simply to find place where they might live in peace and security[1]. It is believed that as the Thangkhals lived amongst the Suktes (Sooties) in the Chin Hills and escaped from the Suktes' control in the Thangkhal village, this Helot race mentioned must be the Thangkhals. It is also believed that the Thangkhals entered into Manipur state in 1877.[2] They entered into the present Manipur state, looking for a place to live permanently. The first known permanent place where they settled in Manipur was at Mulam. From this place, they spread to different places in Manipur especially in Churachandpur district and few of them scattered outside Manipur.

Problem of the Study

The traditional administrative system of the Thangkhals was structurally fabricated by a chief who is known as Hausa as its head. He was assisted in his day to day administration by a council of Elders called Khosung Upa which consists of Manchili, Tangsam, Sikkheng, Siampu and Sawm Upa called the village Youth leader. The institution of Sawm Haam i.e. the Bachelor's

Dormitory where the unmarried males sleep together to meet any unforeseen things played a significant role in moulding the Thangkhal society. The Sawm Haam was under the control of Sawm Upa who was accountable for the administration of the dormitory. Lawmkai, where a group of young men and women work together in the jhum fields by turn was another attractive social practice which became the centre of their community life.

In a patrilineal society like that of the Thangkhals, marriage was solemnized as a bond of family tied. Parents were extremely careful in selecting partners of their children and preference was given to their 'Neita' which means marrying mother's brother's daughter. Marrying Neita was felt important to bring the family relationship more closer. Besides, it also signifies the respect and deep rooted love for their uncle. The first feast prepared by the bride's parent was called Inlam Zonsa, which was as a token for a bride looking for a new house. The peculiar nature of the marriage was that the official wedding ceremony usually took place when the bride was brought to the groom's house and the priest administered the wedding ceremony by tying a bundle of white feathers of a cock around the neck of the bride with words of blessings through incantations.

Among the Thangkhals, the eldest son inherits all the father's properties. The younger brothers and sisters have no share in it. However, when the younger son get married and separated from the father's house, the father or the eldest brother have to give some property to his younger brother who is going to separate from the father's house which is known as 'Intuan'. At any convenient time, the younger brother or the non-inheriting brother after separating from the father's house had to kill a pig and give feast in the inheriting brother's house which is called 'Tousa' (Tou=lord, Sa=meat). It is a means of reciprocating the cares and responsibilities taken by the eldest brother to his younger brothers. After this feast, the non-inheriting brother is really separated from the eldest brother and everything he earns or has is his own now.

It was customary for the Thangkhals to distribute the meat of wild animal. The head, lung, livers and intestines of the animal was given to the eldest brother of the family lineage, the neck portion to eldest maternal uncle, one of the four legs to the village chief and the rest was distributed to the whole villagers known as 'khosung sa'. In this way, it was customary for a Thangkhal to distribute all the parts of the animal killed to the villagers and the hunter had left very few for his family.

The traditional Thangkhal society had various forms of fines and punishments for crimes committed. The fines and punishments depend upon the severity of the crime. The most severe fines and punishments are Sialpi leh Salam which means a fine of a mithun and a pig at the court of the village chief. There was no fine and punishment severe than this in the Thankhal society. Besides this, there was also another fine known as salam leh zubel which includes a pig and a pot of rice beer if the crime is not a severe one. In such fine, the salam would be spend by the chief and his Upas on feast.

With the passes of time, most of the traditional administrative and customary practices have been abandoned. However, many of the practices like marriage price, fines and punishment, distribution of parts of animals killed and many others are still preserved and practiced by them.

Objectives of the study

The main objectives of the present work are:

1. To trace the migratory route of the Thangkhals and their new settlements.
2. To examine the status, power and privileges enjoyed by the early Thangkhal chiefs.
3. To examine the status and privileges enjoyed by the Khosung Upas.
4. To examine in details the customary laws of the Thangkhal tribe.

Significance of the study

Every writing of history has its own significance. The present work also has its own significance for the tribe. As there is no book written and published on the tribe, the present work will be one of the first of its kind which objectively and specifically deals with the traditional administrative system and customary laws of the tribe from research point of view. The scope of the study covers the origin of the Thangkhals, their migratory route, traditional administrative system and their customary law. The people had still practiced many of their customary laws till today.

The present work can be an eye opener to the intellectuals as well as non-intellectuals who are ignorant of the existence of the Thangkhal tribe who has their custom and culture which are different from their cognate tribes. This work could be use by other researchers who are interested on the tribe and will be of immense help for those who are interested on minority group. Some time, the Thangkhal tribe is like a lost tribe who are forgotten by the people though they still exist as a separate tribe. As the tribe is demanding for tribe recognition as a scheduled tribe in Manipur, this present work could be of immense help in this regard for the tribe.

Hypotheses

1. To let it know other people that there is a tribe called the Thangkhals who have their own distinct customs culture, traditions, language which are quite distinct from other tribal groups.
2. Though the tribe has its own custom and culture, there is no authentic record on the tribe for consultation.
3. The chief was the head of the village and as such all the village functionaries were carried under him.

4. The customary laws of the tribe has not been highlighted anywhere. Therefore, attempt is made for an objective study of their culture.

Research design and methodology

Extensive and descriptive research designs have been employed in the present study. As the Thangkhals had no written record in the past, their legends, culture and customary laws exists in oral form. The traditional stories are carried by mouth and words and learnt from their great grand parents from generation to generation. Therefore, primary sources have been mostly employed for collecting facts and information. Some of the gathering techniques are oral traditions, souvenirs, personal interview, magazines and vernacular publications and survey work of the researcher in different places. Over and above these, available secondary sources like published works of the related tribes, journals and periodicals, etc. have also been employed in collecting data and sources for the present work. It also examines the vernacular sources, publication of voluntary organization and associations for any information which can help in establishing the truth of their history and culture.

The methodology for the present work can be stated as historical, interview and analytical. The reason being, the historical origin, migration and settlements of the tribe have been traced through available sources. Thus, historical approach has been utilized as a useful methodology in the present work. Data and facts have also been collected intensively through survey work, oral sources and personal interview of reliable persons and through questionnaires.

Interview has been mainly employed for gathering some of the facts. As a matter of facts, more than 10 aged persons who were well verged in the custom and tradition of the tribe were interviewed. All the data, facts and information which are collected from different sources are objectively assessed and evaluated for arriving at a reliable research finding. Thus, historical, interview and analytical approaches are adopted as methodology for the present research work.

Area of study

The area of the present work covers mostly the state of Manipur. As the Thangkhals are mostly concentrated in Churachandpur district of the present Manipur state, the study has been more or less concentrated in churachandpur district. The study, however, covers the entire state of Manipur and even outside the state where the Thangkhals are living. As the Thangkhals of Manipur had migrated from the Chin Hills of Burma, any political history of the Thangkhals cannot be studied without being tracing from the Chin Hills. Therefore, the origin of the Thangkhals and how this tribe has come into existence have been studied and analysed. Besides, their migratory route from Chin Hills to their present settlements is also studied.

Literature on the tribe and related tribe

The Thangkhals had no literature of their own. The script with Roman characters used by the Paite Tribe is used by the Thangkhals for writing. So, in the absence of the literary evidence for the early period is a conspicuous problem with which we are confronted in the task of reconstructing the history of the Thangkhal tribe. Therefore, the present research project depends mainly on both the oral traditions and the literature of the related tribes. The oral traditional sources include folklores, folksongs, beliefs, ceremonies, superstitions, hymns, rituals, etc. Therefore, a tribe like that of the Thangkhals whose language were reduced to writing only in recent decades cannot be expected to use the conventional recorded indigenous sources as sources for constructing their history for the earlier period. Therefore, the researcher mostly depends on the oral traditions, interviews and questionnaires of some reliable persons. Besides, some research work done on the tribe in recent years like 'The study of the Thangkhal Tribe in Manipur' by Niangdeihnuam, M.Phil. Dissertation, 2008, Manipur University and 'A study of Christianity among the Thangkhals' by Chinminlian, B.Th. Dissertation and some journals and magazines which are related with the tribe are mostly consulted for the work. A part from these, some of the books published by related tribes like 'The Paite, A transborder tribe of India and 'Burma', 1988 by H. Kamkhenthang; 'Discovery of Zouland, 1980 by T. Gougin; 'Zo people and their Culture' 1998 by Singkhawkhai, 'Zo History' 1987 by Dr.Vumson, 'History of the Zomi (Chin) race' 1990 by Vumkhohau; and other related books are consulted to establish the truth of the Thangkhal History. Besides these, there are numbers of work published by Mizo historians and writers which are consulted for the purpose. Above all, the work of other writers especially the colonial writers about the Mizos and Mizoram are also consulted. However, none of the above works give a detail account of the administrative system and customary laws of the people. Therefore, this present work objectively and specifically deals with the traditional administrative and customary laws of the tribe.

Limitations of the study

No authentic research work with regard to the Traditional administrative system and customary law of the Thangkhals has been undertaken. The only available written materials for the tribe are in the form of articles, seminar papers, booklets and few books in the local vernacular language. Not even a single book with proper research work has been published till now.

Therefore, the only materials with which we can depends most in constructing the history and culture of the tribe is on oral sources and those articles and booklets. Besides, as the Government of Manipur did not recognize the tribe as one of the Scheduled tribes of the state, there is no scope for improvement for the tribe. There is no proper record to be found from the state government about the tribe. Therefore, without such records in the area of study, the researcher has been greatly handicapped in gathering data sources. However, with the utilization of the small amount of primary and secondary sources, the work is completed with quite a great hardship. The present work may be lacking in some area of the field and therefore any researcher who are interested on the tribe are mostly welcome to come forward and take the task of research on the tribe and bring out new findings on the tribe.

NOTES

1. Mackenzie, Alexander : *The North East Frontier of India*; Mittal Publications, New Delhi, India, Reproduced- 2007. p 171.
2. Souvenir: *Thangkhal Bible Churh (IFCA-I)*, Silver Jubilee, 1981 2006. p. 4.

CHAPTER 2

Origin, Migration and Early Settlements

Demographic Profile of the Thangkhals

The Thangkhals are one of the many tribes inhabiting the North east India. They belongs to the Mongoloid stock of the Kuki-Chin-Mizo group of tribes. They belong to the Tibeto-Burman family which speaks the Tibeto-Burman languages. They are mostly found in Churachandpur district of Manipur state. All the tribes that consists of Kuki-Chin-Mizo like Zou, Paite, Thadou, Simte, Hmar, Lushai, Gangte, etc. have a common ethnic identity and are very close to each other. However, new trends show that these tribes though having a close affinity with each other are no longer so keen to adopt a common nomenclature now a day. They prefer to be identified by their individual tribal names.[1]

Many tribal groups and sub groups of the Kuki-Chin-Mizo ethnic today claim different from each other on the ground of their language or dialects. Though some of the groups under this were recognized as Scheduled tribe under the Indian Constitution such as Thadou-Kuki, Zou, Gangte, Paite, Vaiphei, Simte, etc, there are still sections or groups of people like the Thangkhals who still claim that they do not belong to any of the above given tribe in respect to their language, custom, culture or tradition.[2]The bulk of their population is found in Churachandpur district of Manipur and many more across the Indo-Myanmar border. This sections or groups i.e. the Thangkhals are so far not recognized as a separate tribe and uncomfortably remain attached to any Zomi tribe for a long time.

Traditional home of the Thangkhals

The original home of the Thangkhals is not definitely known and is still shrouded in obscurity. Scholars have sub-divided Tibeto-Chinese family into sub-group and sub-sub groups and the Kuki-Chin-Mizo (where the Thangkhals are also included) are grouped as Tibeto-Burman family which speaks the Tibeto-Burman language.[3] The original home of these people is not definitely known but somewhere between Kansu in south China and Burma is believed to be their earliest known home.[4] According to Hall, the earliest known home of the Tibeto-Burmese speaking peoples was somewhere between the Gopi desert and north east of Tibet, also possibly Kansu.[5] This region formed parts of southern China where the tribal people are found and widely distributed over the mountainous areas of Kweichow, Szechwan and Yunnan. Specially, Yunnan is found to be the home of tribal peoples.[6] It is believed that the Thangkhals who were also a tribal group might have lived with other tribes in these areas. Thus, the southern China between Kansu and Burma might be considered as the original homes of the tribal peoples including the Thangkhals. There was also a close affinity between the Mizos (Kuki-Chin-Mizo) with the hill tribes of Southern China in languages, mode of living, culture, etc. which leads us to a belief that they came from a common ancestor.[7] It was possible that the Mizos along with non-

Chinese tribes of south China moved down to the south China due to pressure from the Chinese. Thus, in all probability, Swechwan, Yunnan and Kweichow provinces and in wider context, the entire fringed of eastern perimeter of the plateau between Kansu and Burma may be considered as the original home of the Mizo[8] i.e. Kuki-Chin-Mizo including the Thangkhals. Thus, like their other cognate tribes, it is believed that the original home of the Thangkhals might be the southern part of China where the tribals are largely concentrated.

Origin

All societies have their theory of origin. The Thangkhals too, who belongs to the Kuki-Chin-Mizo ethnic groups of tribes have their traditional theory of origin. According to their verbal tradition, the Thangkhals originally came out of a cave which is known as 'Khul' in Thangkhal.[9] The Lushai (Mizos) called it as Chhinlung, the Hmar called it Sinlung,[10] the Paite and the Kukis also called it as 'Khul'. All the Kuki-Chin-Mizo ethnic groups believed in their origin from this cave. But it is hard to believe as fact and it may be absurb to accept as reality that man came out of a cave in this modern world.

However, the tradition of 'Khul' or Sinlung or Chhinlung as the origin of the Kuki-Chin-Mizo groups been kept by all these tribes in various ways such as folksongs, folklore and legends. For people with no writing system, a rich oral tradition was the most reliable means of transmitting past events and collective memories through time.[11] Different groups of the Kuki-Chin-Mizo tribes kept the tradition of Khul or Chhinlung in different versions as the Hmar folklore and folksongs throw some light which depicts that they came out from Sinlung, one of which runs;

Kan Siengna Sinlung ram hmingthang,
Kanu ram ka pa ram ngai,

Chawngzil ang kokir thei changsien,
Kanu ram ka pa ram ngai.[12]

which means

My motherland, famous Sinlung,
Home of my own ancestors.
Could it be called back like Chawngzil.
Home of my own ancestors.

This folk song describes that the people were driven out of their original home-Sinlung or Chhinlung or Khul. It further says that they had a deep attachment to the place. It further says that they wished to go back there if they could.

It is very difficult to identify the exact location of Khul and what it was? According to Hranglien Songate, Sinlung is the present Tailing or Silung in Southwest China. Speculation has also been made that this Sinlung might have been Sining in central China.[13] Another possible theory advocates that Khul (Sinlung) might be the Chinese Emperor Chien Lung and believed that the Kuki-Chin-Mizo were his descendants. It is believed that taking the name of this Chinese Emperor, the Mizos called themselves Chhinlung Chhuak or originated from Chhinlung.[14]

K. Zawla,[15] a Mizo historian put forward the 'Great Wall Theory' in his book 'Mizo Pipute leh an Thlahte Chanchin' for the origin of the Kuki-Chin-Mizo ethnic groups. According to him, Shih Hwang Ti, a cruel king of China followed a repressive policy and started the construction of the Great Wall of China and engaged the ancestors of the Kuki-Chin-Mizo groups.As a result of his repressive policy, the people wanted to leave the place but they could not as they were guarded by the army. But the untimely death of the king led the people to leave the place hurriedly. A song which throws some light on how the Kuki-Chin-Mizo groups hurriedly left the place which ran as;

Khaw Sinlung(Khul) ah

Kawt siel ang ka zuong suok a,

Mile nel lo tam a e

Hriemi hrai a,[16]

meaning,

Out of city Sinlung,

I jumped out like a siel,

Innumerable were the encounters

With the children of men.

From this stanza,we can conclude that the Thangkhals left Sinlung (khul) or the Great Wall of China like a mithun jumping out of the cage.

Among the Thangkhals, Khul occupies the epicenter from where they come out.[17] There are many folk songs and folk lores composed by the Thangkhals which clearly depicts that they lived together in one place called Khul before they came out from the cave. One such song composed by Zamchinhang, Chief of Suangkuang village rans as:

Eiteng khawlkhawm a tuam umlou,

Vannuai chiteng 'Khul' a piang,

Tun sung khat a piang hi ngei ngei e,

Tun sung khat a piang hi ngei ngei e,

Suahpih Sanggam laigui jong khom hi ngei ngei e.[18]

meaing

We the people who are in aggregation are of one stock,

Everybody under heaven is born of a cave,

And born of the same mother

Being born of the same mother,

We all are brothers and are real descendants of the same siblings.

The above statement clearly depicts that everybody under the heaven comes out of cave and all are brothers and are of one family. This shows that everybody that is the Kuki-Chin-Mizo originated from Khul. They are of the same stock and are all brothers. The Chin Hills Gazetteer recorded that there can be no doubt that the Chins and the Kukis are one and the same race, for their appearance, manners, customs and language all point to this conclusion.[19]

It is believed that after the Thangkhals came out of the cave, they lived in China that means this Khul must be somewhere in China. After living for around one hundred years, some went to Tibet, some towards Nepal and some towards Burma.[20] In Burma, they settled for few generations especially in the Chin Hills.

To quote Vumkohau, "Sections of the Chins who have migrated to Burma from the Tibetan Plateaue almost in a straight line down south are to be found from the Somra hill tracts down to Cape Negrais. The Chins, then mostly in North –Western Burma, are known to have had social intercourse with the Burmese at the time of the Kingdom of Pagan (1044-1287). There were Chin levies in the armies of king Bayinaung of Toungoo (1551-81) and of King Alaungpaya of Ava (1752-62)".[21]

He further says that "Local tradition has it that the ancestors of some of the people forming the principal tribes ascended the Chin lands from the Kale-Kabow valleys. One group went there by that foothill Burmese village, Yazagyo, and are the clans now inhabiting the north east region of Teddim. Another group went up Mount Kennedy Peak and settled in Zangpitam above Thuklai village, Sihzang valley. Later they continued their move to Ciimnuai near Sihzang village, Sukte area. Their descendants spread along various routes from Ciimnuai and are believed to be the ancestors of the present tribes of Sihzang, Sukte, Kamhau, Zoute and Thadou.[22] They further moved west and north and spreaded in the present Mizoram and Manipur states.

Thus looking back at the various views and theory put forward for the origin of the Kuki-Chin-Mizo ethnic groups, we can establish on the point that the ancestors of these people once lived in China, Tibet, Nepal and Burma. From proper Burma, they moved towards the Chin Hills and settled in Ciimnuai which may be their first settlement in the Chin Hills. From Ciinnuai the descendants of the Kuki-Chin-Mizo spread in different places.

Early Settlements in the Chin Hills

According to verbal tradition, it is believed that the Thangkhals and their cognate tribe, Kuki-Chin-Mizo ethnic groups came from China. From China, they moved towards Tibet, Nepal and then to Burma. Carey and Tuck suggests that the Kukis of Manipur, the Lushais of Bengal and Assam and the Chins originally lived in what we now known as Thibet (Tibet) and are one and the same stock.[23] In the Chin Hills they lived in different places and it is believed that their first settlement was Ciimnuai. From this place, they spread to different places and founded different villages where they lived in groups.

Ciimnuai Settlement

Ciimnuai may be regarded as the first settlement of the Kuki-Chin-Mizo ethnic groups in the Chin Hills. Here all the cognate tribes are believed to lived together peacefully for a long time. It is believed that Songthu, the legendary led the migration and founded Ciimnuai Settlement.[24] The settlement is situated between the present Saizang and Phaileng villages in the Chin Hills State.[25]

It lies in the eastern bank of the Manipur River enclosed to the west by Lentaang (Innbuk) range and to the east by the Lethar (Thaangmual) range. It is thus hidden from view and looks like a place chosen to take a refuge therein.[26]

Singkhawkhai, a Zo historian says that such old settlements like Geeltui, Saizang, Dimpi, Vangteh, Teizang (Mualbem), Suantak, Kalzang, etc. were founded from Ciimnuai.[27] The Chins, the people living in the northern Chin Hills believed then mostly that their forefathers settled in Ciimnuai, Saizang from where they spread to other places in the Chin Hills. The people called themselves Zoumi. Mi meaning Man. From Ciimnuai some went south and called themselves Suktes, some moved east to the alkah valley Sihzang and later known as Sihzang (Sayin). The Thados branch moved north and some more branch moved west and still called themselves Mizo but known by the British as Lushai (Lusei).[28]

After living several years in Ciimnuai, a discontent arose among the Sihzang and the Thados over the tails of a deer and a flying squirrel. As a result, dispersal took place from Ciimnuai settlement. The Thados left the settlement and founded the Phaileng village, the Sihzang moved to a place near a salt spring and received the name Sihzang, meaning 'near a salt spring'. The Yo too moved out of the settlement and founded a village called Gamngai.[29] From Gamngai, it is believed that a section of them migrated and founded the Taitaam village.

Taitaam

It was the name of a village in which the forefathers of the Thangkhals lived after they came out from Khul and built a number of sequential villages. It was in the Chin Hills and was believed to be founded from Ciimnuai, the first known settlement of the Kuki-Chin-Mizo ethnic groups. After living for several years in this village, some of the villagers shifted to Mualbem (Seizang).[30]

Mualbem

Mualbem was a Sukte village in the Chin Hills under the control of its chief, Khanthuam. Tradition has it that Mualbem and other old settlements in the Chin Hills were founded from Ciimnuai.[31].During this time, most of the Chin Hills was under the control of the Sukte who were the ruling clan. In this village, the Thangkhals, one of the Kuki-Chin-Mizo ethnic groups who do not have their own separate identity by this time shifted from Taitaam village and lived among the Suktes.

One day, few hunters went out for hunting in the deep forest. As they went on, they came to a place where there was a small mountain range which was isolated from others. They then carefully investigated the site for settlement. Being fully satisfied with the site and the surrounding of the place, they decided to shift to that place at the first convenience.

One day after they return, Pu Engseel went to Khanthuam, on behalf of the Taitaam villagers to seek permission to cultivate and administer a portion of land which would prove fruitful and productive.[32] Being approached in an official manner, Pu Khanthuam, chief of Mualbem could not denied the request. Thus, the Taitaam villagers who shifted and lived in Mualbem village among the Suktes moved out of the village and shifted to their newly discovered site of small mountain range that was isolated and started living in it. As the newly founded village was a small mountain range that was isolated, they called it 'Thangkhal'. In their dialect, 'Thangkhal' is composed of two words 'Thang' meaning 'small mountain range' and 'Khal' meaning 'isolated'. Thus, the word 'Thangkhal' which means 'small mountain range that was isolated' was given to be the name of the newly founded village.[33]

Thangkhal Village

Thus, the Thangkhal village was established from Mualbem with the permission of Khanthuam, Chief of Mualbem. In due course, the people from this village developed a distinct culture, traditions and dialects that were different from their cognate tribe of the Kuki-Chin-Mizo ethnic groups. As a result, taking the name of the village, the people called themselves 'Thangkhal'.[34] Thus the Thangkhal tribe came into existence.

In course of time, the Thangkhal village became very prosperous. The Sukte chief, Pu Haupum became envious of its prosperity and sent his brother, Pu Thuamkholian to be the chief among the Thangkhals. As the Suktes were the ruling clan in the area, the Thangkhals could not deny and Pu Thuamkholian thus took over the chieftainship of the Thangkhal village. After Pu Thuamkholiam became the chief, the village was divided into two localities - Boutung (Upper land) and Bounuai (lower land). The Suktes under Pu Thuamkholian settled in the Boutung and the original founder of the village, the Thangkhals settled in Bounuai.[35] Thus, with the coming of the Suktes under Pu Thuamkholian, the village was divided into two localities with two different groups of people which in due course led to the fall of the village and the dispersal of the Thangkhal people.

Fall of the Thangkhal Village and dispersal of the Thangkhal people

There may be many causes for the fall of Thangkhal. One of the probable cause told by the aged people for its fall was the ill feeling which the Thangkhal leaders had against the Sukte Chief, Pu Thuamkholian. During those days, the Thangkhals were good hunter and were fond of hunting wild animals. According to their customary law, the head of the animal hunted down was to be given to the eldest brother of the family or the clan lineage.

But unfortunately, when any animal was hunted down, the Sukte chief, Pu Thuamkholian took away the head portion. Sometimes, he even took away the whole body of the hunted animal, leaving nothing for the hunter. Once Pu Phungseel, one of the Thangkhal leaders hunted a peculiar elephants that have four trunks. The then Suktae chief, Pu Thuamkholian seized the hunted animal and took the credit of killing the animal by himself. This greatly strange the relationship between the two communities (the Suktes and the Thangkhals) and thus exists feeling of great hostility and disharmony.[36]

Another reason can be attributed to the quarrel between the children of Boutung (the Suktes) and Bounuai (the Thangkhals). During those days, the Thangkhal village was divided into two localities - Boutung meaning upper land or locality where the Suktes under their leader, Pu Thuamkholian were dwelling and Bounuai meaning lower locality where the founder of the village,the Thangkhals lived.[37] As days gone by, the children of both the communities often quarreled by shooting one another with slings. The quarrel took such an ugly turn that even the adults were also involved in it. As the matter became worse, the Thangkhal leaders make a secret meeting and plan to leave the village secretly. However this secret plan was leaked and reached the ear of the Chief, Pu Thuamkhlolian.[38] No sooner, when Pu Thuamkholian heard the secret plan of the Thangkhals, he himself went to the Thangkhal leaders and requested them not to leave the village. As a token of love and means of pleading them to stay, Pu Thuamkholian offered a big earthen pot of rice beer and killed a pig at the residence of Pu Thahvum,one of the great Thangkhal leaders and persuaded them not to leave the village.[39]

Though the request of Pu Thuamkholian was genuine and respectful, the Thangkhals in heart decided to leave the village at the earliest convenience. One day, at an early hour of dawn, every household of the Thangkhal community destroyed their ovens and started secretly leaving the village, once for all, leaving behind their immovable properties and moved towards the North West.[40]

When the Suktes under Pu Thuamkholian heard about the dispersal of the Thangkhals, some of them decided to pursue and killed them all. At this juncture, Pu Thuamkholian, the Sukte chief pleaded his people not to pursue or else the Thangkhals under Pu Thahvum, Pu Phungsel, Pu Lingtut, Pu Zagen who were sharp shooters will not remain silent and they all will be killed. Besides these people, there are more than 10 sharp shooters who can cause trouble to them. As a result of this request, the Suktes stopped pursuing the Thangkhal peoples.[41]

After leaving the Thangkhal village, the people leaded by warriors of sharp shooters and a number of strong and sharp shooter guarding from the rear move forward towards India and crossed the Imphal River, leaving the Chin Hills once for all. The Suktes under their chief, Pu Thuamkholian pursued upto the Imphal River. When they reached the bank of the river, Pu Thuamkholian, at the top of his voice shout and persuaded the Thangkhals to return back and promised to live together peacefully. The Thangkhals who were on the other side of the river turned down the request made by the chief by saying the they never return back to the place where they had destroyed their ovens.[42] Thus in grief, Pu Thuamkholian returned back to the old Thangkhal village, waiting chance to come back among the Thangkhals.

Places of Settlements in Manipur:

After they left the Thangkhals village, the forefathers of the Thangkhals crossed the Imphal River at Tuithang and entered into Manipur, India. They travelled through different place to reach their first permanent settlement in Manipur at Mulam in the southern part of Churachandpur district. During these periods, they travelled through these places:[43]

(1) Teddim

(2) Tuithang.

(3) Ngaljang

(4) Suangsang

(5) Philnah

(6) Talek

(7) Nivangtang

(8) Singgial

(9) Khodam

(10) Aisih

(11) Siallutak

(12) IIiangtam

(13) Hiangtamjang

(14) Sialna

(15) Paldai

(16) Thangkhal Lamtun

(17) Tuitha

(18) Takheu

(19) Tanmun

(20) Thonghau Thangpi kot

(21) Tuaiteng vum (Gallamtang)

(22) Mulam

They came across all these place under the leadership of Pu Thahvum[44] and started settling permanently at Mulam which might be the first permanent Thangkhal village in Manipur, India. From this place, the forefathers of the Thangkhals spread in different directions in Churachandpur district of Manipur and set up different villages under different leaders called Hausa (chief)

Mulam

Mulam may be said to be the first place where the Thangkhals first settled permanently in Manipur. While moving in search of permanent place for living, the forefathers of the Thangkhals saw an eagle casting a lot. The Thangkhals believed that the place where an eagle cast a lot will be suitable and good place for settlement. As such, they named the place 'MULAM' meaning eagle casting lot and settled in the place.[45]

While the Thangkhals were living peacefully and comfortably in this village, Pu Thuamkholian, the Sukte chief of the Thangkhal village along with some of his villagers came and arrived at Mulam unexpectedly. As the Suktes were the ruling clan under whom the Thangkhals were once, the Thangkhals could not deny the claim of Thuamkholian to be the chief of Mulam. As such, Pu Thuamkholian once again becomes the chief of Mulam.[46] In course of time, the Thangkhals began to move in different directions and settled in different places and founded different villages in Churachandpur district. Some of the villages founded by the early Thangkhals and their descendants in Manipur are:

(1) Mulam.

(2) Tuallian.

(3) Sialkawng.

(4) Tuidam.

(5) Nahjang.

(6) Khuainuai.

(7) Khaukual

(8) Tanglian.

(9) Khuangkhai.

(10) Suangkuang.
(11) Bualjang.
(12) Sialnah.
(13) Siallutak.
(14) Hiangtam (K)
(15) Kamkeilon.
(16) Tuibuang.
(17) Khuangmun.
(18) Ngoiphai.
(19) Saiboh.
(20) Mutei Khaukual.
(21) T. Khajang
(22) Teikot.
(23) Phaisan.
(24) Gilgal.
(25) Singheu.
(26) Teisaljang.
(27) Gangpimual.
(28) Joalphai.
(29) Kotlian.
(30) Belbing.
(31) Geltui.
(32) Munhoih.
(33) Geltam.
(34) Kullian.
(35) Phaisat.
(36) Tuining.
(37) Hita.

(38) Daktum.

(39) Buangmun.

(40) Suangjang.

(41) Muallum.

(42) Kamhang

In most of the above villages, the descendants of the Thangkhals still settled and called themselves as 'Thangkhals'. But unfortunately, many of them are ashamed to be called themselves as Thangkhal even though they are descendants of the people who came from Thangkhal village in the Chin Hills of Myanmar, might be the Thangkhals are still very backward or the Thangkhals are not recognized as a separate tribe in Manipur or both combined together. Unfortunately, those who did not want to call themselves as Thangkhal decided to attach themselves to any one of the Kuki-Chin-Mizo group. However, there are many who still preferred to called themselves as Thangkhal and stand on the dictum 'Our dialect is our identity' because they have their own dialect called 'Thangkhal Ham' (Thangkhal language), customs and culture which are quite distinct from their cognate tribes and are still running for tribe recognition under the Indian Constitution. What the Thangkhals needed now most is Tribe recognition from the Government so that it can save this minority tribe or else the tribe will be extinct.

NOTES

1. Rualkhumzo: "Traditional Administrative System and Customary Law of the Hmars in Manipur"; Ph.D. Thesis (unpublished), Department of Political Science, Manipur University, Canchipur, 2004, p.1.
2. Niangdeihnuam: *The Study of the Thangkhal Tribe of Manipur, M.Phil. Dissertation* (unpublished), Department of History, Manipur University, Canchipur, 2008, p.4.
3. Gierson,G.A.; *Linguistic Survey of India*, Vol.III, Part III, Motilal Banarsidass, Delhi, 1967, pp.3 & 10.

4. Souvenir; Mizoram College Teacher's Association Silver Jubilee (1978-2003), p.11.
5. Hall,D.G.E.; *A History of South East Asia*, Macmillan Co. Ltd., London, 1955, p.123.
6. Sangkima; Mizos: *Society and Social Change*, Krishna Kumar Spectrum Publication, Guwahati, Assam, 1992, p.13.
7. *ibid.* p.14.
8. *ibid.*
9. Souvenir; Thangkhal Bible Church (IFCA – I), Silver Jubilee Celebration, 1981 – 2006, p.1. (Hereafter cited as Thangkhal Bible Church).
10. Pudaite, Rochunga; *The Education of the Hmar People*, Indo-Burma Pioneer Mission, Sielmat, Manipur, 1963,p.1.
11. Sakhong,Lian H; In: *Search of Chin Identity; A study in Religion, Politics and Ethnic Identity in Burma*, Nordic Institute, Second Print, 2008, pp. 1 & 2.
12. Pudaite, Rochunga; *op. cit.* p.1.
13. *ibid.* p. 21.
14. Lalthangliana, B; *Mizo Chanchin*, RTM Press, Aizawl, 2001, p.23.
15. Zawla, K.; *Mizo Pipute leh an Thlahte Chanchin*, Lengchhawn Press, Aizawl, 5th Edition, 2001, pp. 6-7.
16. Songate, L. *Hranglien; Hmar Chanchin* (Hmar History), Enlarged and published by Rev. T. Khuma Songate, Churachandpur, Manipur, 3rd Edition, 1996, p.13.
17. *History of the Thangkhal People's Organisation*, Published by Thangkhal People's Organisation, 2003, p.1. (Hereafter cited as Thangkhal people).
18. Khaikhanthang interviewed.
19. *The Chin Hills Gazetteer*, 1896, Chapter XII 135, as quoted by Vumkhohau in his book *History of the Zoumi (Chin) Race*, Zougam Research Publications, Lamka, 1990, p.1.
20. *Thangkhal People*, *op. cit.* p.1.
21. Vumkhohau; *History of the Zoumi (Chin) Race*, Zougam Research Publications, Lamka, 1990, p.2.
22. Vumkhohau; *op. cit.* p.1.
23. Tuck, H.N. and Carey, Bectram S; *The Chin Hills*, Tribal Research Institute, Aizawl, Mizoram, Reprint, 2008, p. 2.
24. Singkhokhai; *Zo People and their Culture*, Published by Khampu Hatzaw, Churachandpur, Manipur, 1995, p.17.
25. Niangdeihnuam; *op. cit*, p.13.

26. Singkhawkhai; *op. cit.* 14.
27. *ibid.* p.73.
28. Vumkhohau; *op. cit.* pp. 1-2.
29. Vumson; *Zo History*, published by the Author, Aizawl, Mizoram, 1996, p.76.
30. Niangdeihnuam; *op. cit.* p. 14.
31. Singkhawkhai; *op. cit.* p. 73.
32. Chinminlian,T.; A study of Christianity among the Thangkhal Community, B.Th. Dissertation (unpublished), Asian Baptist Bible College, Bible Hill, Rengkai, Churachandpur, Manipur, 2011, p.2.
33. Thangkhal People, *op. cit.* p.3.
34. Upa Thangchinkhai interviewed.
35. Thangkhal People, *op. cit.* p.3.
36. Niangdeihnuam; *op. cit.* pp. 17-18.
37. Thangkhal Bible Church, p. 3.
38. Chinminlian, T.; *op. cit.* p.3.
39. Thangkhal People; *op. cit.*, p.4.
40. Niangdeihnuam; *op. cit.*, p.19.
41. Thangkhal People; *op. cit.*, p.5.
42. *ibid.*
43. Ginzahang interviewed.
44. Thangkhal People; *op. cit.*p.4.
45. *ibid.*, p.6.
46. *ibid.*

CHAPTER 3

Traditional Administrative System

Introduction

Before the coming of the British, the tribal societies of the North East Indian had their own traditional administrative system. They had evolved and maintained their own system. However, the system of administration among the different tribes differed from tribe to tribe and from region to region.[1] V. Venkata Rao says that authoritarian type of institutions existed among the Chin-Mizo-Kuki groups, the Singphos, the Khamtis, the Riangs, etc.[2] The Thangkhals too had evolved an administrative system of their own, slightly different from other tribal groups in many aspects. The day to day administration of the village was carried out by the chief, help by his councilors called Khosung Upas. They carried out law and orders of the village. This present chapter is an attempt to give an elaborate account of the traditional administrative system of the Thangkhals of Manipur.

The Village

The Thangkhal village is perched on the top of the hill or a ridge. It was done to defense themselves from the tribal conflicts and warfare which threatened the existence of the village. The Thangkhals were very careful in selecting the site of their village. Before finally selecting the site of their village, a group of selected elders will go and sleep one night at the proposed site, bringing a cock with them and if the cock did not crow before dawn, the site would be considered not suitable and if the cock crow before dawn, it would be considered suitable for settlement.[3]

The Thangkhals would carefully investigate the proposed site for their village before shifting there. Importance would be given to the availability of enough land for jhum cultivation, good defensive position it command in tribal war or its impregnability against every attack combined with a good perennial source of water supply. After being fully satisfied with the surrounding and the atmosphere of the place, the Thangkhals would settle down and formed a village comprising of 20 to 30 houses.[4] During this time, living together in a cluster was felt important to defense themselves from tribal conflicts and warfare which threatened the existence of every tribal village. Thus, a Thangkhal village was set up under the leadership of one person called 'Hausa' who was the head of the village. Mostly, the Thangkhals lived in their village with their kids and kins.

When a Thangkhal village was set up, it is a must to have a chief who is called 'HAUSA' whose post is not elective but hereditary and is passed on from father to his eldest son, who otherwise is known as 'Upa'.[5] Without a chief, no village can be establish. It was the chief who established or founded the village and have the supreme power in the village. The chief was helped in his day to day administration by a few selected elders of the village which consists of the village cabinet called 'Khosung upa' and the village youth leader called 'Sawm upa'.[6] The chief and his cabinet will decide all the things happened in the village and all decisions are taken by them and their decisions will be final and binding to all the villagers.

The Chief

'Hausa' is a Thangkhal word for chief. The chieftainship was a hereditary institution.[7] The chief was the founder of the village. Theoretically, all the powers in the village belong to the chief and he is a despot. But in practice, he administered the village as advised by the village council who are selected by the chief from the people whom he favoured. He had also the right to dismiss any of his Upas at any moment without assigning any reason thereof.[8] He presided over the meetings of the council which were generally held in his house.[9] Decisions were usually taken by the consensus of this council.[10] However, he usually rule the people according to the customary law of the Thangkhals as his subjects can desert him if he rule despotically and move to other village as they were free to move and shift to any village as they wish. This check on his power, however, did not diminish the importance of the chief in his village.[11]

A Thangkhal chief was succeeded by his eldest son that is his legitimate son. If he has no legitimate sons, his eldest Meita (Hmeifa) succeeds to his village.

Powers and Functions

The Thangkhal chief was responsible for the control of the village administration. He along with his councilor's works for the welfare of the villagers.The welfare and security of the people were the prime concern of the chief. It was the duty of the villagers to obey the orders and decisions of the chief with his councilors. All matters relating to the issue of orders, framing of rules and regulations and important instructions were made by the chief and his councilors based upon the customs and traditions of the people. Those who disobeyed were punished and even expelled from the village.[12]

A Thangkhal chief was responsible for taking care of the poor, orphan, widows sick and any needy people in the village. He has to provide food and shelter to those people. He also had the right to receive and protect any criminal who take shelter in his house. By accident or intentionally, if someone killed another, to escape punishment, such persons can take shelter in the chief's house[13] and no one can harm him until his case was heard in the chief's court and final decision was made.

The chief was also empowered to work as the dispenser of social justice in his village. His court functioned as the highest legal authority in the village.[14] Cases like murder, theft, adultery, seduction, etc. are settled by the chief and his councilors. His verdict was final and binding on both the parties.[15] The council can discuss any matter. It tried both civil and criminal cases. The appellant would bring a jar of rice beer at the court as a court fee to file a law suit. Only after this, the council including some of the elder people in the village will discuss and decide the case. In such cases, if any member of the council including the chief had any connection with the impending case, they did not participate in the deliberation, nor would interfere with the findings or decisions.[16] The council was the only court and there was no other court of appeal. The court will take up all the cases and its decision was final and binding on the people. The village court acted as a court of compromise within the society.[17] After the case has been heard, the court imposed fine upon the guilty party. A fine of Salam (a pig) and zubel (a pot of rice beer) was imposed on the guilty party according to the customary law of the Thangkhal if the case is not serious. However, if the case is a serious one, the guilty party will be fine Salam, zubel and

Sialpi (a mithun). The mithun will be given to the winner party. The chief and his Upas-the elders would usually spend the salam on a feast.[18] The salam and the zubel are the privileges enjoyed by the council. However, all these are done not to hurt any party but to bring compromise among the parties in particular and in the society in general.

In a Thangkhal village, the chief was virtually the proprietor of the entire village land called Gam.[19] It was his duty to makc allotment of lands for house building and cultivation among the villagers in consultation with his councilors. If anyone from other village wants to migrate to the village, he or she has to ask permission for settling in the village from the chief. Again, the chief also has the power to banish any subject from his village if they do not obey the rules and regulations of the village and he can also confiscate all the properties.[20] In such cases, all the confiscated properties will be taken by the chief.

It was also the duty of the chief to welcome distinguish visitors to the village. He has to take care of the visitors during his or her stay in the village.[21] It was also his duty to provide food, shelter and safety to the visitors during their sojourn in the village.

In the traditional Thangkhal village, the chief with his councilors looked after the administration of the village. Theoretically, all the powers are vested in the chief. He decided all the cases in consultation with his councilors. All the village officials like the Manchillis, Tangsam, Sikkheng, Siampu were appointed by him. They all together worked for the welfare of the village.

Privileges of the Chief

A Thangkhal chief had certain privileges for looking after the village. As he was busy in looking after the village administration, he has some privileges. All that the village contains belongs to the chief and he can call upon his people to furnish him with everything that he requires.[22] The privileges enjoyed by the Thangkhal chief in his village are:

Saliang

It was the right leg of an animal killed or caught in trap by the villagers in jungle hunting. It was a must for every villager to give this saliang to the chief.[23] In case the villager failed to pay this tax, he had to pay a fine of sialpi (a mithun) and salam (a pig) as compensation to the chief.[24]

Tangseu

It was a paddy given by the villagers to the chief every year which was a basket full made of bamboo which was about 3 tins. The amount may differ from village to village. It was likely that the Manchilis and widows were exempted from this due. Those who do not pay Tangseu will be find Sialpi and Salam by the chief.[25] For giving Tangseu, a particular day was fixed. On that particular day fixed, the villagers will bring the fixed amount of paddy to be given to the chief. In return, the chief will feed the whole villagers with rice beer called Tangseu zu or Buh seu zu in return for what he got from the villagers by way of tax. His councilor also contributes or donates pots of rice beer on this day.[26]

Manual labour **(Free construction of house)**

An important right of the chief was to have his house built by the villagers without payment of any cost either for labour or collection of building materials when his house needs to be repair or newly constructed. For this, at least one person from each household will come for constructing the chief's house. It was, however, customary for the chief to give a feast to the villagers when the house was completed.[27]

Limitations and check on the chief

Theoretically, the chief enjoyed enormous powers in his village. He was all in all in the village and no one can question on his authority. However, in reality, his powers were not without any limitation. He has to act according to the customary laws. If he becomes too tyrannical, his subjects may leave and migrate to other village and seek shelter under another chief.[28] They have the right to migrate to any village of their choice. Even if the chief did not allow, he could move stealthily in the night.[29] As his power also depend on the number of houses in which he rule, he have to look for the welfare of the people and should not become too tyrant. He should also take into account the advice and opinions of the councilors who were there to help him in any decision making. Sometimes, if the chief was inefficient and incompetent, there were chances of reducing him to almost a puppet and his councilors really rule him.

Thus, in return to the services rendered by the villagers, free of cost and the tributes paid as token of loyalty, recognition, obedience and solidarity, the Hausa has to protect their interests by providing security socially, politically and economically. It is also the bounded duty of the Hausa to see that every villager is protected from external aggression and danger.[30]

The village officials

The chief in a Thangkhal village have authority over all the village functionaries. In the discharge of his day to day duties, the chief was assisted by a council of elders called Khosung upas. It consists of the two Manchilis, the Taangsam, the Sikkheng, the Siampu[31] and others appointed by the chief, depending on the size of the population of the village. The chief appointed his council from amongst those who were rich, well-informed, broadminded, influential persons and from his near relatives in the village.

Manchilis (Deputy Chief)

The Manchili was the first cabinet member of a Thangkhal village. There can be one or two manchilis in a village.[32] If there are more than one Manchilis in a village, one of the Manchili will be appointed as the main Manchili, to be next in power to the chief. They were appointed by the chief. Their main duty was to help the chief in his day to day administration. They help the chief in the administration of justice in the village, accompanied the chief when he went for tour, assist the chief in the distribution of cultivable land among the villagers annually, receptions of visitors from outside the village. In short, we can say that the Manchilis were there to help the chief in any needed situation.

Privileges

As a reward in recognition to their work, the Manchilis enjoyed the following rights and privileges:

1. They were given the solid flesh portion of the hind leg called 'Sakhuailu' by the villagers when they killed or trapped animals.
2. They were exempted from the payment of paddy due called Tangseu to the chief annually.
3. They were exempted from forced labour or community services rendered by the villagers.
4. They are given the first privilege next to the chief every year to select site for jhum cultivation.
5. He along with other councillors were entitled to share Salam which was imposed on the loser party when a case was settled in the village court.[33]

Tangsaam (Announcer)

The Tangsaam was the village crier who was appointed by the chief. Every Thangkhal village had a Tangsaam. He was to announce to the public the orders passed by the chief and his councilors to the villagers. He also carried messages to the Upas and others. Every resolutions passed by the village council was made known to the Tangsaam who in turn passed it on to the public by shouting at the top of his voice while walking through each and every land inside the village.[34] All the announcements were usually made by the Tangsam at night. Besides, he was also to inform all the members of the council whenever a meeting of the councilors was to be held.

Privileges

The privileges enjoyed by the Tangsaam are:

1. He was exempted from Tangseu which was a paddy due payable to the chief.
2. He was also exempted from rendering compulsory community service.
3. He received a small amount of paddy from each house hold annually.
4. After cases were decided in the village court and feast was thrown with the fine imposed on the loser party which was called Salam, the Tangsaam also joined the councillors in the feast.[35]

Sikkheng (Blacksmith)

The Sikkheng or the village blacksmith was another important official of the Thangkhal village. He was appointed by the chief. His main duty was to make and repair the agriculture tools as well as any other tools for the villagers. As the early Thangkhals were agriculturist, he was one of the most important and needed person in a Thangkhal village. His workshop was in his veranda called Sumtong. However, there were also other blacksmith who were not appointed by the chief. The number of blacksmiths in the village depends upon the size of the village but it is usual to have one or two in a village.[36] Thus, there were official blacksmith appointed by the chief and also private blacksmith, not appointed by the chief in a village. Villagers are not bound to get their tools repaired by the official blacksmith but can go to a private blacksmith to repaired their tools if they like. The blacksmiths made and repaired various agricultural implements like Tem (dao), Hei (axe), Tu (hoe), Phiau (sickle), etc.

Privileges:

1. He was given two (2) kerosin tins of paddy which was called Pumhai every year by those who are attached to him. This Pumhai was given to him after he prepares the pumhai zu for the villagers at the end of the year.
2. He was also given the sikkheng sa (meat) by those who are attached to him if they shot or trapped animal.
3. He was exempted from Tangseu, an annual paddy due to the chief.[37]

Siampu (Priest)

The Siampu or the priest was an important official in the Thangkhal traditional society. He was the village priest who was appointed by the village chief for performing all kinds of ceremonies for the villagers. Any kind of illness was supposed to cause by evil spirits and sacrifices were required to propitiate the spirits. The village priest diagnosed the illness and prescribed appropriate sacrifices for the illness.[38] He must be available at all times to all the families in the village for any sacrifices. Without him, no sacrifices can be made. He acted as intermediary between the people and god or gods inside the society.

The Siampu was regarded as the representative of God on earth.[39] He was believed to know all the sources of problem and illness caused by the spirits and the types of sacrifices to be made to appease the spirit. As such, he acted as a mediator between men and the objects they worshipped and performed the sacrifices. The forms of sacrifices and mode of performances differ for every spirit according to the nature of the illness. In his capacity, the official Siampu performed sacrifices on behalf of the whole community at least once a year.

The number of Siampu in a Thangkhal village was not the same. In a village, there must be at least one Siampu appointed by the chief who was the official Siampu. Besides him, there can be a number of Siampu in the early Thangkhal village.[40] The villagers are free to go to any Siampu (priest) of their choice whom they thought could cure their sickness if they are sick.

To become a Siampu, one has to know all the religious beliefs and practices of the Thangkhals as well as have the qualities of a sorcerer, a seer or a prophet.

Functions of the priest

The Siampu in a traditional Thangkhal society played a very important role and performed number of functions. The functions can be divided into two:

Judicial functions

The judicial function of the Siampu was to decide difficult cases which the village councils could not decide. Any complicated case which could not be decided by the village court was referred to the priest for his decisions. In such cases, the Siampu used to decide the case by administering an oath in which both the parties concerned would undertake it. In such cases, the party concerned was some time asked to bike a tiger's tooth or ammunition.[41] Before they bite it, the Siampu recite chant and both the party concerned will swear in the name of God if they were telling lie, they will be bitten by tiger or they will be kill by gun. Thus to know the culprit, the Siampu used such method.

Another method adopted by the Siampu to decide complicated case was by Aitui Don. [42] Under this system, the Siampu will prepared Aitui (Ai juice) from some Ai plants and asked the parties concerned to drink the Aitui. In such cases, it was believed that the one who tell lie will die after drinking the Aitui whereas nothing will happen to the one who tell the truth and he or she will survive.

Another way of deciding complicated case was by Tuilut which means immersion in water.[43] Under this system, the Siampu will lead both the parties for competition in immersion in water where there is water. Before the competition begins, both the parties will select the best swimmer to represent them. The Siampu then will recite the chant and the competition will begin. In such kind of competition, the one who tell the truth can immersed in water and can stay longer period whereas the one who tell lie cannot stay in water and afloat on the water even though he might be the best swimmer. It was believed that in such cases of trial, Pasian, their God stands as witness.[44]

Another way of deciding complicated case by the priest was by drinking water through the barrel of the gun. In such cases, the Siampu shall put water in the barrel of the gun and led it drink both the parties swearing that he or she speaks the truth.[45] It was believed that the one who tell a lie will die of gun's shooting. Thus, in the traditional Thangkhal society, the Siampu played a very important role in deciding complicated cases which the chief and his councilors could not decide. In most of the cases decided by the Siampu in such ways, the culprit was known.

Sacrificial Functions

Kithoih is a Thangkhal word for sacrifice. According to the Thangkhal Customary Law, when a person was sick, the Siampu (Priest) will looked after the sick person and advised what kind of sacrifice to be performed. The family members of the sick person believed what the priest had said and performed any kind of sacrifices as was advised by the priest. Without the priest, no sacrifice can be performed. There are different forms of sacrifices performed by the priest for an individual as well as for the general public. Some of those sacrifices performed by the priest may be briefly described below:

Zanlam

Zanlam is a sacrifice performed when a person suffers from pain in the joints, bones, chest, etc. The priest would advice the person to perform the sacrifice. The priest himself performed it and used pig or dog or any other animal to perform the ritual. The priest with his helpers will go to the outskirt of the village called 'Khuamual' and perform the sacrifice by killing the animal and cooked and eat the meat. At the advice of the Siampu, a bunch of leaves was hung in front of the house of the patient and before the fixed day as advised by the priest, the bunch cannot be removed. During that period, they cannot entertain any guest; otherwise it will spoil the sacrifice. As they believe in the sacrifice, they were usually healed from their sufferings.[46]

Bangtung

Those persons suffering from pain in the chest, cough, bones, joints, body, etc are called Bangtung. The priest performed the sacrifices and for it they used a dog. The dog's blood was mixed up with wine and grounded spices. The priests then make the chants and let it drink the patient.[47] In this way, the Bangtung sacrifice was performed.

Gamlian

The Thangkhal forefathers believed that those who suffered from intense high fever are said to have suffer from Gamlian. The priest with his helper would take a pig or a goat and make the sacrifices at the outskirt of the village. They hung a bunch of leaves at the front of the house of the patient. As they believed in the sacrifice, they were healed from the diseases. In today's context, Gamlian disease must have been malaria which was caused as a result of mosquito's bite.[48]

Gam Nupi

A person suffering from fever, headache, etc are believed to be suffering from Gam Nupi. The priest with his helpers will perform the sacrifices and used a piglet or a dog to appease the evil spirit which is believed to cause the illness. In this way, Gam Nupi sacrifice is performed and they were healed from their suffering.[49]

Dailam

Dailam is a disease mainly suffered by children below the age of 15. They mainly suffered from cough, chest pain, fever, etc. For those who suffered from such disease, the priest used to performed sacrifice at the outskirt of the village called 'khuamual' with his helper using a piglet. There are two types of dailam sacrifices:

(a) **Kaihkhup**: A child suffering from Dailam and bend his head down are called kaihkhup.

(b) **Kaihdak**: A child suffering from Dailam and stay his head in upright position are called Kaihdak. Though Dailam is divided into Kaihkhup and kaihdak, the disease which they suffered are the same and the sacrifice performed by the priest was also the same. There was no difference at all in the treatment of the disease.[50]

Siam Kithoih

In Siam kithoih, they used hen or a cock. The priest would sacrifice hen of odd number for example 1, 3, 5, 7... A cage called siambom was made from bamboo and in it, they kept the beak, legs and all the intestine of the hen killed. After the meat was eaten, the priest will keep away the Siambom at an isolated place.[51]

Kinel Buh

Kinel Buh is a kind of sacrifice performed by a priest when a person had a bad dream about someone else or when someone was very ill. The priest would performed the sacrifice by killing a buffalo, cow, mithun or any other animal and would pray for the well being of the patient.[52]

Kausia Khiang khoh

It was performed when a person suffered from stomach ache, sudden fall while standing and unwilling to speak to anyone. The priest will perform the sacrifice.[53]

Gamkau

When a person suffered from dysentery and passed stool and also vomits often, they are said to be suffering from Gamkau. The priest will perform the sacrifice so as to cure the patient. In today's context, the disease referred here must have been cholera combined with typhoid.[54]

Mamut

Those people who suffered from injured in the jungle by wild animals, injured at home from hot water, burnt, broken bones and others are said to suffer from Mamut. The priest would blow softly at the injured place to cure the patient.[55]

Tuilut

Tuilut means dipped in water. It was believed that some patients are believed to be caught by the spirits of water. In such cases, the priest will take the patient to the jungle where there was a stagnant pool which is believed to be inhabited by evil spirits or demons to dip in the pool to please the evil spirits. Such sacrifice is called Tuilut in Thangkhal.[56]

Loulut

The Thangkhal forefathers believed that if there is a stagnant pool of water in their paddy field, the place is believed to be inhabited by evil spirits which can cause harm to them. In such case, the priest would make sacrifice at the place to please the evil spirits. Such practiced was called Loulut. Lou means field and Lut means dip. So, it is freely translated as making sacrifice at the field to please the evil spirits.[57]

Sumtawng/buh thoih

Sumtawng is a Thangkhal word for a place of grinding rice in a house. The forefathers of Thangkhals worshipped their gods in such places, praying for abundant blessings to have a good harvest. Animals like piglet, pig, chicken, and boar are used for making such sacrifices. It is believed that at this Sumtawng, the old woman mentioned in the folk tale 'Thanghou leh Liando' who looked after the two brothers had disappeared and this sacrifice was offered to please that old waman.[58]

Inn sung

When a person suffered from Gamlian and could not be cure easily, the Inn sung sacrifice was performed. The priest would perform the sacrifice by killing a cow or a buffalo. In such sacrifice, they would worship the 'Sutzung which means the main pillar of the house. At the main pillar, the priest would perform the sacrifice by citing chants and will pray for the recovery and good health of the patient.[59]

Hisia kithoih

Hisia in Thangkhal means a common diseases suffered by women (taina, pangna, nauneih a kawngna etc.). In such cases, the priest would perform sacrifice for healing the diseases.[60]

Buak

Buak means a sudden occurrence of things on a person. For example - a sudden illness on a person while working at the field, or in the forest or while going on the way and such things are called Tuakmi. When a person suffered from such illness, they treated in such a way that they will take a leaf of tree on the left and right of the road and would put over each other and with that, they will led the patient drink water which is called Buak leh. Besides, they will make a Chiampek (used in weaving clothes) and at the tip of it, will tied a thread and poured water over it and led it drink the patient those drops of water dropping from the loose end of the thread. Some of the patient who are lucky enough will get healed. However, most of the patient cannot be heal by performing such practices. Such illness was mostly caused by gamkau.[61]

Salai Aat

Salai Aat sacrifice is performed by a priest when a person suffered from such illness like stomach ache, ulcer, etc. concerning with stomach ache. In such sacrifices, a piglet will be kept over the patient and with some incantations; the priest will cut at the stomach of the piglet. Such sacrifice is called Salai Aat.[62]

Sakham veite kithoih dan

The early Thangkhals make sacrifice for those Sakham vei by killing a dog or a hen. It was performed by the priest in front of the house.[63]

Khawbawl

Khawbawl means praying for the well being of the villagers by the priest. According to the Thangkhal Customary Law, a particular day of the year was observed by the whole villagers by remaining in their own respective house and no one was allow to go out on such day. This day was observed by the villagers for the well being of the villagers. On such day, priest would distribute toys of mithun and coins made of mud or clay to every house. As the Thangkhal villages were inhabited by people of various sub-clans, an arrangement was made in such a way that the head of every families from different sub-clans and helper known as Tuanvai to make the number odd would be brought together for example 1-3-5-7-9- and so on. The priest along with his friends would then proceed at one end of the village and made sacrifice to their gods for the good health and well-being of the villagers. In this way, Khawbawl is usually done by the early Thangkhals al least once in a year.[64]

Nauphit

According to the Thangkhal custom, when a person had more than one children, to show their gratitude, the maternal uncle would bring pork to the house and also would bring a garland made of hen's or cock's feather and garlanded the children and blessed them. In return, the uncle would be given a sum of Rs 3/- and an axe by the nephew. Then, thc axc would be place over the top of rice beer and would sprinkle rice beer over the axe by the mouth. The maternal uncle would bless the child to be tough and healthy by saying '*sik bang in dam inla, sik bang in hong tak in*' which means 'be healthy like iron and be strong like iron'. This kind of practices followed by the early Thangkhals was called Nauphit.[65]

Bum

According to the Thangkhal custom, an illness caused on a person as a result of the use of black magic is called bum. This bum is usually done to take revenge on other person. It has different symptoms like vomiting of blood, ulcer, etc. It can be cure by a priest or a man who is having black magic. However, those who are going to cure the illness must be much better than those who do the black magic. Otherwise, he or she could not cure the black magic. To treat such kind of illness, they will erect all types of wood around the house, keeping a distance of about Lam thum which may be 15 feet in between the end of every two poles. They will fix a certain type of creepers having thorns on those poles. Then the priest who would make the sacrifice would dance at the top of the house roof, tapping the bottom of a dog and chanted the magical words. After that, he will throw down the dog and they will kill the dog. They would led the patient drink the dog's blood. All sorts of spices were tied together and they will place them along with the dog's head on the top of the gate. In such way, they tried to cure those patients who suffered as a result of Bum and some of them were cured and some of them cannot be cure.[66] Thus, the Siampu played a very important role in sacrifice to cure the sickness of the villagers.

Privileges enjoyed by the Siampu

In return for his service to the people, the Siampu enjoyed the following privileges:

a. Whenever sacrifice was made with four-footed animals, he was given the fore- legs of the sacrificial animal.

b. He was exempted from Tangseu (paddy tribute given to the chief).

c. He also had the right to collect a certain amount of paddy annually to the villagers who were attached to him for any sacrifice.[67]

Sawm Haam (Bachelor's dormitory)

Sawm Haam is a Thangkhal word for the bachelor's dormitory. It was the nerve-centre of the Thangkhal society which shaped the Thangkhal youths into responsible adult members of the society. In the early period, the Bachelors of the Thangkhal village built a big house in front of the chief or the Khong-Toupa's house which is called Haam in which all the bachelors sleep together to meet any unforeseen things.[68] There can also be more than one Haam in a village depending on the size of the village. Sometimes some of the children were also allowed to sleep in it. Visitors from other villages were also allowed to sleep and spent the night in the Sawm Haam.[69]

The inmates of the Sawm Haam were divided into three categories: Sawm Upa, Sawm Tangval and Sawm naupang. Among the three inmates, the Sawm Upa was the most powerful one.

The Sawm Haam was placed under the charged of a leader called Sawm Upa (Val-Upa). He was chosen among the inmates of the Sawm Haam based on seniority, courage and efficiency in hunting and organizational activities.[70] All the inmates of the Sawm Haam were under his control. He was accountable for the smooth administration of the dormitory and also to the chief and his council members. He assumed the commanding post and commanded the youth in any warfare.

The inmates of the Sawm Haam were responsible for the welfare of the village. They sleep at the Sawm Haam together at night to meet any unforeseen things that were to happen. In the evening, most of the Sawm Tangvals went out in the house of the ladies for courting and will come back at late night to sleep there.[71] They also used the Sawm Haam as a recreation centre. They used to practice wrestling and many other things in the Haam at night before they went out for courting. Sometimes, they also have wrestling with guest from other village who wanted to sleep in the Sawm Haam. Besides this Saam tangvals, the Sawm Haam also had one junior group composed of young boy's known as Sawm Naupang. Their main duties were to supply the Sawm Haam with fire wood every day.[72] If they fail in their duty, they can be punished by the Sawm Tangvals. In short, the Sawm Haam was a very powerful institution which exercised the greatest sway in establishing social norms and customs among the early Thangkhal people and shaped them into responsible adult members of the society.

The Sawm Upa or the youth commander was selected from the inmates of the Sawm Haam according to their seniority in age and experience in various administrative sphere. His post was a coveted one. He was accountable for the administration of the Sawm Haam. However, his term ceased as Sawm Upa once he got married and then new Sawm Upa will be elected.[73]

The Sawm Upa, being the leader of the Sawm Haam looked after the welfare of the youths and their dormitory. He was responsible for organizing the group to take up definite responsibility over the village and it was customary for every Sawm Haam dwellers to obey him. He was assisted by a number of lieutenants who were assigned with the charge of day to day vigilance and service of the village.[74]

The Sawm Haam served as a place where the young boys were looked after. Since there was no school during that time, they started learning many things from the dormitory. They learned about the art of wrestling, code of conduct, etiquette, hunting, etc. Under the guidance and supervision of the Sawm Upa, they were made aware of their customary laws and practices.[75] The inmates also have at least few rounds of wrestling bouts under his guidance which was compulsory for all the inmates.

Being the Youth Commander, the Sawm Upa assigned different duties to the youths to be performed when someone died in the village. He select and sent some people as sikou (messenger) to give the news of the death to their relatives and friends who were in other places. He also selected the site for the grave and advised the youths to dig the grave.

Tawmngaihna or self sacrifice which was one of the most valued traits of the early Thangkhals was also imparted to the youths by the Sawm Upa. Under his guidance, the youths were always ready to surpass their friend in chivalrous act and bravery in any emergency. To be ready for such emergency, some have never really slept for fear of not being able to be the first one to wake up at the first sign.[76] The youths were also always ready to show their Tawmngaihna for the cause of the community welfare. For instance, if someone was unable to finish his jhum land due to sickness or some misfortune, the Sawm Haam mates along with the young girls from the village rendered a helping hand and finished the remaining work.[77]

The Sawm Upa assumed the commanding post in the Sawm Haam. In times of war, he mobilized the Youths and becomes the youth commander and commanded them in the warfare. All the youths under the guidance of Sawm Upa slept together at Sawm Haam and kept their weapons ready for use to meet any unforeseen. Sawm Upa also trained the youths in times of peace in different arts.

Thus, the Sawm upa (Val Upa) played a great role in the traditional Thangkhal society by moulding the life of the youths who were the future leaders of the society. It was under his guidance and supervision that the youths were trained and imparted leadership qualities and developed among them.

Sawm Haam Sa

It was a feast throw to the inmates of the Sawm Haam by the wife of the Khawng- Toupa or the chief at the end of every year. They killed pig and prepared feast annually. In this way, they made marry making every year at the end of the year.[78]

Lawm (village Labour corps)

The word 'Lawm' means an informal labour organization in a simple and corporate village life of the Thangkhals wherein all the able-bodied young boys and girls are members.[79] It is concerned mainly with the economic life of the village. All the able bodied young boys and girls formed a group and work in the jhum fields by turn. The number of work attended by a Lawm member will be credited to his name and the same number of work he thus earns will be repaid to him by other members with labour. Sometimes, the Lawm members will help those who could not finish their jhum fields due to unavoidable circumstances like sickness or due to death. This Lawm became the centre of the Thangkhal's community life. After they all completed the work by turn, they held a festival of 'Lawm Zu' where they drink zu and enjoyed merry making by singing and dancing the whole night.[80]

Sawm vawk

According to the customary law of the Thangkhal, they reared pig every year by rotation and at the end of the year, those pigs were killed and throw feast at the house of the Khawng Toupa by the whole villagers. They will take the meat with zu and spent the day with much gaiety.[81] They used to sing the traditional song called Sannemla.

Sawmzunek and Sawmsanek

The Thangkhal forefathers had celebrated annually at the end of harvest festival called Sawm zunek and Sawmsanek. Sawm zunek means drinking of zu by the whole villagers and Sawmsanek means eating of meat by the whole villagers. On this day, all the villagers will bring pots of zu and drink the zu the whole day and night. Besides, all the Sawm vawks were killed and a feast was prepared for the whole villagers.[82] They will sing the traditional songs called Sannemla for the whole night and dance.

NOTES

1. Ruolkhumzo: *Traditional Administrative System and Customary Law of the Hmars in Manipur*; Unpublished Ph.D. Thesis, Department of Political Science, Manipur University, Canchipur, 2004, p.81.
2. Rao, V. Venkata : *A Century of tribal politics North East India, 1874-1974;* New Delhi, S. Chand & Company Ltd., 1976, p.103.
3. Henchithang Zou interviewed.
4. History of the Thangkhal People's Organisation Published by Thangkhal People's Organisation, Lamka, Manipur, 2003, p.21.(Hereafter cited as Thangkhal People).

5. Gangte, T.S: *The Kukis of Manipur: A Historical Analysis;* Gyan Publishing House, New Delhi, 2003, p.125.
6. Ginzahang, interviewed.
7. Rao, V. Venkata, Gangte, T.S & Devi, Ksh. Bimola; *A Century of Government and Politics in North East India; Vol. IV- Manipur*, S. Chand & company Ltd., Ram Nagar, New Delhi, 1991, p.41.
8. Sangkima: *Mizos: Society and Social Change*; Spectrum Publications, Guwahati, Assam, 1992, p.37.
9. Malsawma, H.L: *Sociology of the Mizos*; Spectrum Publications, Guwahati, Assam, 2002, p.15.
10. Hluna, J.V: *Education and Missionaries*; Spectrum Publications, Guwahati, Assam, 1992, p.11.
11. Sangkima, ed.: *Modern History of Mizoram*, Spectrum Publications, Guwahati, Assam, 2004.p.2.
12. Rualkhumzo: *op. cit.*, p. 84.
13. Rao, V. Venkata, Thansanga, H.& Hazarika, Niru; *A Century of Government and Politics in North East India; Vol. III - Mizoram*; S. Chand & Company (Plt.), Ltd., New Delhi, 1987, p. 65.
14. Nunthara, C: *Mizoram: Society and Polity*; Indus Publishing Company, New Delhi, India, 1996, p. 74.
15. Sharma, Vijay Prakash: *The Hmars of Manipur*; Anthropological Exploration, New Delhi, Anmol Publications, 1992, p.37.
16. Khamsuanpau interviewed.
17. Niangdeihnuam: *op. cit.*, p. 31.
18. Ralte, Benjamin & Malsawmliana, ed: *Social, Economic and Political History of the Mizos*; EBH Publishers, Guwahati, 2011, p. 46.
19. Upa Thangchinkhai interviewed.
20. Rao, V. Venkata; *op. cit.*, 65.
21. Niangdeihnuam: *op. cit.*, p. 32.
22. Chambers, O.A: *Hand Book of the Lushai Country*; Tribal Research Institute, Aizawl, Mizoram, Reprint-2005, p. 68.
23. Kampau Mate interviewed.
24. Rao,V. Venkata, Gangte, T.S. and Devi, Ksh Bimola; Vol. IV; *op. cit.*, p. 42.
25. Thangchinsuan interviewed.
26. Chinminlian, T: *A study of Christianity among the Thangkhal Community*; B.Th. Dissertation (unpublished); Asian Baptist Bible College, Bible Hill, Rengkai, Churachandpur, Manipur, 2011, p.13.

27. Chatterji, N: *The Earlier Mizo Society*; Tribal Research Institute, Aizawl, Mizoram, Second Reprint-2008, p. 45.
28. Rao, V.Venkata: *op. cit.*, p. 65.
29. *Paite in Mizoram*: Tribal Research Institute, Aizawl, Mizoram, 2011, p. 33. (Hereafter cited as Paite).
30. Gangte,T.S.: *op. cit.*, p.127.
31. Upa Thangchinkhai interviewed.
32. Khupchinkhai interviewed.
33. Ginzahang interviewed.
34. Rualkhumzo: *op. cit.*, p.118
35. Ginzahang interviewed.
36. Ralte, Benjamin & Malsawmliana: *op. cit.*, p.12.
37. Ginzahang interviewed.
38. Nunthara, C., *op. cit.*, p. 67.
39. Lunzahau interviewed.
40. Lunzahau interviewed.
41. Rev. Khupkhochin interviewed.
42. Henchinthang Zou interviewed.
43. Thangchinsuan interviewed.
44. Upa Thangchikhai interviewed.
45. Ginzadal interviewed.
46. The Thangkhal People: *op. cit.*, p.39.
47. *Ibid.* P.40.
48. Niangdeihnuam: *op. cit.*, p.40.
49. Rev. S. Khaisuanmang interviewed.
50. Thangkhal People: *op. cit.*, p. 41.
51. Rev. Khamchinhang interviewed.
52. Ginzahang interviewed.
53. Thangkhal People: *op. cit* p.41.
54. Thangkhal People: *op. cit.* p. 42.
55. *Ibid.*
56. Upa Thangchinkhai interviewed.
57. Rev Khamchinhang interviewed.
58. Thangkhal People: *op. cit.* p. 42.
59. *Ibid.* p.43.

60. Lunzahau Interviewed.
61. Thangkhal People: *op. cit.*, p. 43.
62. *Ibid.*, p. 44.
63. *Ibid.*
64. Rev. Khamchinhang interviewed.
65. Thangkhal People: *op. cit.*, p. 44.
66. *Ibid.*, p. 45.
67. Ginzahang interviewed.
68. Thangkhal People: *op. cit.*, p. 30.
69. Chingzanian interviewed.
70. Niangdeihnuam: *op. cit.*, p. 34.
71. Thangkhal People: *op. cit.*, p. 30.
72. Niangdeihnuam: *op. cit.*, p. 33.
73. Rev Khamchinhang interviewed.
74. Mate, S.Haukhanlian: *Social and Religious transformation among the Mizos (1891-1972);* Ph.D. Thesis (unpublished), Department of History, Manipur University, Canchipur, 2005, p. 67.
75. Rualkhumzo: *op. cit.*, p.114.
76. Mate, S. Haukhanlian; *op. cit.*, p. 68.
77. Niangdeihnuam; *op. cit.*, p.34.
78. Souvenir: Thangkhal Sinlai Pawlpi, *Sinlai Suangphum* (1987-2008), p. 106. (Hereatfer cited as Sinlai Suangphum).
79. Gangte, T.S.; *op. cit.*, p.132.
80. Niangdeihnuam; *op. cit.*, p.34.
81. Sinlai Suangphum, p. 106.
82. *Ibid.*

CHAPTER 4

Customary Laws

Introduction

From time immemorial, the Thangkhals living in different parts of North East India were having their own customary law which dealt with their individual and social life. There were customary laws which deal with marriagc, divorce, inheritance, death, crime and punishment, etc. These customary laws served as the law of the land and everyone was bound to obey it. Even the chief and his councilors were not exceptions to it. The present chapter is an attempt to study the customary laws and practices of the Thangkhals which are discussed as under the following heads:

Marriage System

'Kiteng' is a Thangkhal word for marry. The institution of marriage occupies an important place in the Thangkhal society. It is the backbone of their society which brings the family relationship more closer. Basically, marriage among the Thangkhal was a civil contract, soluble at the will of both the parties concerned.[1] Normally, it was arranged by the parents. The parents exercise utmost care and solemnity in the selection of a life partner of their children. They did not look only at the outward character and accomplishments for the partner of their children. They carefully enquire into his or her lineage. Many characteristics such as insanity, epilepsy, talkativeness, thieving, laziness, etc are considered hereditable and the children of such persons are not like by the parents for their children.[2]

Traditionally, monogamy was the common form of marriage among the Thangkhals. Polygamy was not common. However, as time passed on, some of the chief and few others began to have a secondary wife called 'Mei'[3] and practiced polygamy in spite of its condemnation by the society. The legitimate wife or the first wife is called Zipi and the concubine or secondary wife is called Mei. Those 'Mei' did not however, occupy the same status with the first wife[4] and the status of the Mei is much lower than the Zipi. According to the Customary Law of the Thangkhal, the eldest son of the Zipi will inherit his father's property and the Mei's son had no share in it.

Marriage is an important form of institution among the Thangkhals. Free mixing of boys and girls are allowed but pre-marital sex relationships are not common.[5] For selecting their life partners; great importance was attached to the relationship of the mother's brother's daughter and sister's son in the Thangkhal society. This system gives the sister's son certain special rights over mother's brother's daughter known as his 'Neita'. The relationship between mother's brother and sister's son may be described as follows:

(a) Sister's son (uterine nephew) is the object of special attention on the part of his mother's brother. (maternal uncle)

(b) As a prospective son-in-law, the sister's son is at liberty to do or take anything he likes, including taking food as he pleases in the house of his mother's brother who gives unlimited indulgence to him.

(c) Sister's son has a rightful claim on the daughter of mother's brother, his 'Neita'.

(d) Mother's brother has an obligation on his sister's son about giving marriage of his daughter to him.

(e) Sister's son is bound by custom to marry mother's brother's daughter.

(f) Mother's brother is bound to give his daughter to his sister's son in marriage.[6]

Traditionally, there are two types of marriage among the Thangkhals - arranged marriage and elopement.

Arranged Marriage

This type of marriage is socially and customarily a recognized marriage among the Thangkhals. As marriage among the Thangkhals was a civil contract made at the consent of both parties concerned, the parents will arranged the marriage. They were not restricted to any particular clan or family. A man can marry almost any women except his sister, aunt, mother, grandmother. They were also restricted not to marry the sisters of their brother-in-law (sisters husband). If they marry the sister of their brother-in-law, it is called *Luang ki khek* and it was not permitted by the Thangkhal custom. However, preference was given to cross cousin marriage that is marrying mother's brother's daughter called *Neita*. This kind of arranged marriage often takes place during the childhood of the boy and the girl. When the parents of a boy were determined that their son should marry no other than his mother's brother's daughter called Neita, the marriage negotiations is initiated by the parents of the boy during the childhood of the boy and the girl. In some extreme cases, when a daughter is born in a family, her father's sister and her husband initiated on her birth the claim that the baby girl being the 'Neita' of their son, should not be given in marriage to anybody else. She should go to them as their son's wife. Such earmarking is called 'Ki khau khih' meaning that the girl has been reserved for a particular boy and that no one should set his eye on her, either for marriage or for love.[7] The girl is the most eligible and suitable for the boy to marry. The boy is expected to marry his Neita to bring the family relationship more closer. It also signifies the respect and the deep rooted love for their uncles.[8] As marrying the Neita was the expected law of marriage among the Thangkhals, if anyone involved in the marriage process and married the Neita, he will be accused of *'Sial Khau Sattan'* (cutting of the mithun's rope) which literally means separating one's affinity and will be legally sued with a fine of "*Sialpi leh Salam*" (a fine of mithun and pig)[9]. Thus, no one was allow to interfere in the marriage proposal of the Neita.

Elopement

Another type of marriage which prevailed among the Thangkhals was elopement. This type of marriage was socially and customarily unrecognized. It takes place when both the boy and girl fall in love but their parents did not consent to the marriage or when there appears a third person in between the boy and the girl who is likely to stand in their way, because of being a serious contender to win the hand of the girl in marriage or when the economic consideration that involves in the event of all formalities of marriage are to be fulfilled in the case of either the boy or the girl being in abject poverty, or even when the girl is impregnated by either of the lovers. In all these cases, marriage by elopement is resorted.[10] For this type of marriage, courting was done and in the process, both the boy and girl felt in love with each other without the consent of their parents. As the parents did not consent to their marriage, the boy elope with the girl. The young man and the girl who was in love would secretly go to some other village and get married without the consent of their parents and hide themselves from the girl's parents. This was regarded as disgraceful for the girl.[11] The first duty of the boy's family was to send their mediator to the girl's parents to apologise and report the elopement of the girl and request to consent the marriage. If the girl's parents are not willing, they can take back the girl even though she has lost her virginity.[12] After negotiations were made, the couple will come back to the boy's house. This type of marriage may be called love marriage.

Marriage proposal

The method of finding a partner for a boy was traditionally regulated by the boy's parents. The boy's parents usually sent their mediators called their '*zawl*' and '*tanupi*'[13] to the girl's parents with a jar of *zu* for initial negotiation when their son was marriageable age. If the girl's parents drank the *zu*, it was taken as they accepted the proposal and further negotiations follows.[14] Usually the boy's family will send their mediators for three times. In the process, the girls were hardly asked anything about their opinion. If the parents were convinced about the suitor, she was bound to accept the proposal. However, in certain cases, the girls were asked about their opinion and if she accepts it, she will just said as you wish but if not, she can also reject the proposal. In many cases, both the couples never knew or meet each other before they married.

Bride Price

Bride price exists among the Thangkhals. Customarily, the bride price was fixed as 'Sial Nga' (five mithun).[15] Though it was fixed as five mithun, it did not necessarily stick to mithun alone. It can also be paid in money. If it is to be paid in money, it depends on the mutual understanding of both the parties. They can even pay Rs. 10 or Rs. 100 as equal to a mithun if there is mutual understanding or else it may be very high.[16] The marriage price can be paid in easy installments and can last for a very long period.

Marriage Ceremony

After all the arrangements were ready for the marriage, the palai handed over the marriage price on behalf of the groom to the girl's parents and the marriage contract was made. The girl's parents then will arrange a feast called 'Inlam Zonsa'[17] as a token for a bride looking for a new house and usually the whole villagers were invited to the marriage feast. In the evening, the bride will be brought to the groom's house by her relatives.[18] The official wedding ceremony usually takes place when the bride was brought to the groom's house. For this, the priest would administer the wedding ceremony by tying a bundle of white feathers of a cock around the neck of the bride with words of blessings. This was done to introduce the bride to the 'Pusa' (house hold god) of the groom and to accept her as their own family member from that day onward.[19] Thus, in this way, the wedding ceremony was celebrated among the early Thangkhals.

Mouvan Ken (Dowry)

When a Thangkhal girl married, she takes some materials to her husband's houses as dowry. Some materials are compulsory while some depends upon the capability of the bride's family. Some of the compulsory materials are:

1. *Seu 1 (a basket made of bamboo),*
2. *Nam 1 (a strap made of cane meant for carrying seu),*

3. *Puandum 1 (a traditional shawl),*
4. *Tutang 1 (a hoe),*
5. *Heitang 1(an axe),*
6. *Zanpuan 1 (a woven rough blanket made of cotton).*[20]

Besides the above mentioned compulsory materials, a bride can also take any materials in kind or in cash to her husband's house. Some of the materials specially clothes and utensils are distributed among the near relatives of the groom. However, all these materials depend on the capability of the bride's family and are not compulsory.

Tunsaa

According to the customary law of the Thangkhal, a feast prepared in honour of the bride by her family was called Tunsaa.[21] Generally, the bride family was to kill three animals compulsorily for Tunsaa but not necessarily at a time. They can kill one or two or three animals at a time depending on their convenience. On such occasion, they will give away the head, both fore and hind legs, hip and the chest portion of the slaughtered animal or animals to the family of the son-in-law. With the remaining portion, they will throw a feast. This Tunsaa was one of the most important things to be done when a Thangkhal girl married.

Sasengsin

When animal or animals are killed on the occasion of Tunsaa, the meat which are given to the family of the son-in-law are kept in a basket known as Seu and was usually covered with a shawl or any kind of cloth. Such shawl or cloth is called Sasengsin.[22] This Sasengsin will be owned by the one who carried the Seu.

Pusum

According to the customary law of the Thangkhals, it was compulsory for the groom to pay a sum of Rs 3 to the maternal grandfather or if he is not there to the eldest maternal uncle of the bride which is called Pusum.[23] Perhaps, *Pu*, the brides' maternal uncle is the most important person to get a share of the marriage price.[24] If this is not given, a boy cannot marry a Thangkhal girl.

Tha-man

According to the Thangkhal custom, when a woman married, the groom had to give a sum of Rs 3/- to the mother of the bride which was known as Tha-man.[25] This was given to the mother as a reward for looking after her daughter.[26] This Tha-man was compulsorily given to the mother of the bride.

Sial Ak Mat

Acccording to the Thangkhal custom, when the groom's party paid a mithun or money as marriage price of the bride to the girl's family, they will in return give a cock or a sum of Rs 10 with a shawl to the groom's party. This was called Sial Ak Mat.[27]

Thus, the Thangkhal marriage system was different from many of their cognate tribe though it looks like very similar. Their preference to cross cousin marriage known as marrying their Neita was a peculiar one which was to bring the family relationship more closer with their maternal uncles. It also signifies their respects and deep rooted love for their uncles. Taking of the bride price, Thaman, pusum and other in the process of the marriage are not to meant to sell the girl or to gives burden to the groom but to make good relationship between the couple and their families. This Thangkhal marriage system may have many similarities with many of the tribal groups especially with those of Manipur but a critical study will reveal many of its difference.

Divorce

Kikhen is a Thangkhal word for Divorce. Among the Thangkhal, divorce occasionally occurred though it was strongly condemned by the society. There are two types of divorce among the Thangkhals:

A Husband Divorcing his wife:

If a husband wants to divorce his wife according to the Thangkhal Customary law, it is done as follow:

a) He must give a mithun as a fine to the family of his wife,

b) He must return back all the things brought by his wife as dowry at the time of marriage,

c) He cannot make claim of whatever he had paid for the marriage price instead he should paid up all the balance of the marriage price if he did not clear up.[28]

A woman leaving her husband:

According to the customary law of the Thangkhals, if a woman wants to leave her husband, it is done in the following manner:

a) She has to return back the whole of the marriage price that her husband had paid to her relatives.

b) All the things brought by her as dowry at the time of marriage must remain with her husband and she cannot make claim on it.

c) She also cannot made claim at anything she had acquired while staying with her husband.

d) Nothing will be said and discuss about all the animals slaughtered and all the *zu* drank in her favour in the process of her marriage.[29]

Besides the above mentioned types of divorces, if a husband divorces his wife having a child, according to the customary law, it should be done as follow:

a) The mother should take care of the child for a period of three years or till the child reach the age of three. During that period, if the child is sick or ill, all the expenditure on medicine and any other things will be borne by the father.

b) After the expiry of three years, the father can claim the child by paying a mithun to the mother.

c) If the father refuses to take the child after the expiry of three years, the child is to remain with the mother and uncle and automatically became a part and parcel of the family. However, in many cases, when the child got maturity, he himself took his father's title and not his mother and become part of his father's family.[30]

Widow Remarriage

The traditional Thangkhal society permitted widow remarriage. Widows often re-marry and there is no law or custom preventing them from it.[31] However, if the widow desire to remarry, she should disaffiliate herself physically and spiritually from the deceased husband's clan first and rejoin her natal clan.[32] If a woman has a son and there is any property, it is proper for her to remain unmarried and look after her son and his interests. However, if she wishes to remarry, there is nothing to prevent her, but her deceased husband's relatives (inheriting brother) will take charge of the children and all the properties.[33] If the woman has children and decided to live in her deceased husband's house, she was permitted to do so. However, in such condition, she is considered as still married to her deceased husband and if she is detected in an intrigue, it is considered tantamount to adultery which was greatly objectionably to the members of the deceased husband's family. In such case, the widow was to leave her deceased husband's house and her relatives will have to refund her marriage price just as if her husband was alive.[34] Such kind of act was shameful and derogatory on the part of the woman.

Ukanman

Ukanman is something like a compensation given to the elder sister if her younger sister married before her. Usually, the early Thangkhals takes one mithun for this.[35] It was to be given by the groom's parents.

Adultery

'Adultery' in Thangkhal means Angkawm. It is considered a great disgrace for a woman to be caught in adultery. If a married woman commits adultery either while her husband is alive or after his death while she is still in her husband's house, she was considered to be Angkawm. There are two kinds of adultery which are governed by the Thangkhal customary law.

The first one is adultery during the life time of her husband and the second is adultery after the death of her husband. According to the Thangkhal customary law, such woman should be dealt in the following manner:

1) The person who commits adultery with the woman should be fine Sialpi leh Salam.
2) If the husband did not accept his wife any more, the husband is permitted to divorce his wife without returning the dowry. If the couple divorce on this account, the man responsible for it should refund the entire marriage price to the former husband which he had paid to the relatives of his wife.
3) If the person who commits adultery with the woman married her, the entire marriage price and other necessary

things should be re-decided.

4) If the man responsible for this is already married and on this account if his wife left him without the man divorcing her, they should divorce as it is without any fine on each party which is known as Ki Ak Gualkhen.

5) If the woman is pregnant on this account, the man should return the entire marriage price to the woman's husband which he had already given to the woman's relatives. If the man responsible for it did not married the woman, she should look after the child for three years after which the man should take the child by paying a mithun to the woman's relatives.[36]

There is also another type of adultery which a man can commit. If a married man commits adultery, he should be dealt in the following way:

a) He should be fine Sialpi leh Salam.

b) If they have child, the mother should look after the child for three years after which the father should take the child by paying a mithun.

c) During those three years, if anything happen to the child, the father should take all the responsibilities to look after the child.[37]

There is also another type of adultery which is called Zi Lak Sak which means eloping with someone's wife. If a man elopes with other's wife, he should be dealt in this way:

a) He should be fine Sialpi leh Salam.

b) He should refund all the marriage price to her husband which he had already paid to the woman's relatives

c) The woman marriage price should be re-decided.

d) He should pay the court fee.[38]

Numei Sual (Rape)

Inside the traditional Thangkhal society, if a man violated the chastity of a woman without her consent but through the use of force, it was called Numei sual (rape). Even mere attempt to rape was taken to be very seriously and the culprit was to be fine. Normally rape among the early Thangkhals was very rare and if any complaint was brought to the notice of the chief and his councilors, the matter was taken very serious and if the accused was found guilty, he should be fine as follow:

1. He should be fine zubel (a pot of rice beer),
2. He should pay court fee,
3. He should be fine sialpi (a mithun) and salam (a pig),
4. After rapping, if the man did not marry the woman, he should be fine five mithun.[39]
5. Further, if the victim got pregnant, the mother had to look after the child for three years after which the father had to take the child after paying a mithun to the mother.

Zawlta (Illegitimate child)

Zawlta means illegitimate child. Any illegitimate child should be look after by the mother for three years after which the father should take the child by paying a mithun. During those three years, if the child is ill or anything happen to it, all the responsibility will be borne by the father. After three years, the father has to take the child by paying a mithun.[40] Even though they are the illegitimate child of the father, if the child is a male and the eldest son of the father, he can claim to inherit his father's property.[41]

Zawlgai (pre-marital pregnant):

If a man and woman have pre-marital sex and if the woman got pregnant, it is called zawlgai in Thangkhal. A child born of such wedlock is known as Zawlta. They were very much looked down upon in the society and were considered as a great disgrace for the family. This was not like by the early Thangkhals and specially the woman were no more like by man to marry again. Whenever there was a case of such illegitimate pregnancy of a girl, the man responsible for it had to marry the woman. In such cases, if the man did not marry the woman, he has to fine the following:

a) Sialpi leh Salam (a mithun and a pig; the pig is to be slaughter for feeding the court member),

b) He should pay court fee (Innpi sap),

c) The mother should look after the child for three years after which the father should take the child by paying a she mithun. During that period, if anything happen to the child, it will be the responsibility of the father.

d) If the mother died during her pregnancy or due to child birth, the man responsible for it should wrap the dead body with a traditional shawl, he should kill a pig or a cow on the day which is called Kawsa Sa and he should also be fine a mithun and a pig.[42]

Zawlgai ta lalou

If a man and a woman have pre-marital sex and if the woman got pregnant and the man did not want to marry or did not take the child, it is called Zawlgai ta lalou. According to the Thangkhal Customary Law, such person should be fine:

(a) a mithun.

(b) A jar of rice beer.

(c) the mother should look after the child for three years.

(d) After three years, the father should take the child by paying a mithun.[43]

Meisia

Meisia in Thangkhal means having more than one wife or practicing polygamy. This was strongly opposed by the Thangkhals and is regarded as disgraceful. In spite of its opposition, some of them have concubine. If a man have concubine, he should be fine a mithum which is known as Suanman to be given to the relatives of the first wife. It is a must and he must pay at once.[44] If the first wife returns back to her parents, they should divorce as it was without returning any dowry or without returning the entire marriage price which the husband had already paid which is known as 'Ki Ak Gual Khen'.

Mouluah (marrying elder brother's wife)

Mouluah in Thangkhal means marrying elder brother's wife after the death of elder brother. If a married man dies, any of his surviving brothers who are not already married has the right to marrying the widow of the deceased.[45] The widow can refuge but usually she accepts.[46] If a man marries his sister-in-law in such way, he has to give a mithun as a fine to the father-in-law. After giving a mithun, the woman's family should compulsorily kill an animal.

Tagah Khawi

'Tagah' means orphan. Therefore, 'Tagah khawi' means looking after orphan. If a child become orphan due to the death of his or her parents, they are to be look after by their eldest paternal uncle who would inherit the property or if he is not there, the eldest son of the paternal uncle. However, if the child wants to stay with their maternal uncle, they are allowed to stay as long as they wish. However, if anything happen to the child, it would be the responsibility of the paternal uncle or the one who would inherit the property. In such cases, the maternal uncle could not claim anything for being looking after the child from the paternal uncle.[47]

Gamluah (inheritance)

'Gamluah' in Thangkhal means inheritance. According to the customary law of the Thangkhals, the eldest son of the father would inherit his father's properties. After the death of the father, his eldest son would inherit the properties and would become the head of the family and will look after the family. If a man has no legitimate son to inherit his property, Meita (son by a concubine) can inherit. If he has no Meita, Zawlta (illegitimate son) can claim to inherit his father's property. Again in the absence of a son, the heir is the nearest male of a man on his father's side.[48] Thus, in the Thangkhal society, inheritance was only through the male line and women cannot inherit.[49] Whether the son is legitimate or illegitimate, the eldest son of the father inherits his father's properties.[50] At the same time, if his younger brothers die without any male issue, he would inherit all their properties and took the responsibility of looking after his family members. However, if the wife of his decease brother did not remarry or did not go back to her parental home, the eldest brother cannot inherit the property.

Buluh

Buluh means going to one's house for fighting. If a person went and beat another person in his own house, he should be fine as:

1. (a) A pot of rice beer and Salam (salam means a big boar which would be kill and eaten by the court members),

   (b) Court fee,

   (c) A mithun.

2. In the course of fighting, if the man dies, he should fine;

   (a) A pot of rice beer,

   (b) Killed an animal as kawsa sa on the day,

   (c) One traditional shawl,

   (d) Court fee,

   (e) Ten mithuns,

   (d) Some amount of money agreed upon between by the two parties.

3. If he hurt the person, he should look after the wound of the person and should bear all the expenses. Besides, he should also be fine as 1.(a), (b) and (c) above.[51]

Khut Khial

According to the customary law of the Thangkhals, murder cases are classified into two categories - accidental and intentional. If a person killed someone accidentally, he should cover the dead body with a Thangkhal traditional shawl called puandum. He should also be fine a pot of rice beer and a mithun.[52] He should also pay the court fee. Besides, he should also killed an animal which is called kawsa sa.[53] If there is any other fine to be imposed, it should be decided by the chief and his council and that should be accepted by both the parties.

On the other hand, if a person killed someone intentionally, he should be fine:

(a) A pot of rice beer.

(b) Court fee.

(c) Killed an animal on the day as kawsa sa,

(d) One traditional shawl to wrap the dead body.

(e) He should be fine 5 mithun.[54]

Besides, if there is any other fine to be imposed, it should be decided by the chief and his councilors

Nauzaw Inntuan (Younger brother having separate house)

A younger brother, after married, he should move out of the main house to have a separate house for himself which is known as 'Inntuan'. Whenever, the younger brothers move out of the main house, the eldest brother should give different articles like utensils, clothes, house, etc. which are necessary for his brother to start a new life with his family. The younger brother has to content himself with whatever he was given by his eldest brother and he cannot complain it.

Naming of a child

According to the customary law of the Thangkhals, naming of a child took place within three to seven days after the child birth. They had very peculiarities in naming the child. Like some of their cognate tribes in Manipur - the Thadous, the Gangtes, the Vaipheis, the Simtes, the Zous, etc., the Thangkhals also have a distinct rigid naming system which has a unique place among social systems all over the world.[55] Usually, the first son and daughter were to be named by the paternal grandparents whereas the second son and daughter were to be named by the maternal grandparents respectively. Their names were usually composed of three syllables - the first syllable of the child's name took the last syllable of the one who gave the child's name. Each of the three syllables had their meanings for example - let us take the name Hangkhanpau. The one who gave his name is said Kamchinhang, his grandfather. The first syllable of the child 'Hang' is taken from the last syllable of his grandfather, Hang. Then the middle syllables 'Khan" signifies his youth age and the last syllable 'Pau' means famous or strong or one who can do things. This kind of naming made it very easy for assessing the genealogy of a child or a person. The system of naming among the Thangkhals like the Kukis is peculiar - unique in its system. The naming system is so strong that even after generations it still holds way in the society and can maintain their genealogical tree for generations.[56] All the meanings of their names signify their grandparents' greatness, fame, strength or any other things which they wanted to show or reveal to others. So, naming of a child among the early Thangkhals was taken very serious and they are throwing some parties while making this ceremony.

Ngabendan (Fishing)

The early Thangkhals were very fond of catching fish. They used different materials to catch fish. Usually they used *Ngen, Lemu*, stick and *dao* to catch fish.[57] Besides, they also used *Gu, Leigu, Phok* (poisonous fruit, roots) etc. for catching fish. When they are to catch fish, on the night before going out to catch it, they will announced that the next day the whole village will go for catching fish. They will also announce the place where they will go for catching. Everyone who go for catching fish will bring their materials like *Gu* and *phok* and also catching equipments like *ngen*, *lenta* and others. They will mixed their materials like *gu, phok* and others with water and throw it in the water. When the fishes drink the water, they will be intoxicated and became drank and then they will catch the fishes. Whatever they catch, they will share equally among themselves.

Besides this, the early Thangkhals also made *ngoi* to catch fish. This can be individually or can be done by two or three persons jointly. Whatever they catch, they will share among themselves and if it was done by a single person, he will have all the fishes he catches.

Gamvakdan (went for hunting)

From the beginning, the Thangkhals were fond of hunting animals. They are competing each other in hunting animals and having of paddy. They went for hunting individually or in group. When they went individually, they will just sit in one place where they believed the animal will come. On the other hand, if they go in group, those who bring gun will go and stay at a far distance and the rest will make line and spread in the forest and move towards the persons who bring guns and wait for the animals to come. They will sought and move towards those who have guns so that the animals will run in front of them which will be shoot by those who bring gun who were known as Tangpang. Those who sought in group were known as Tanghol. Sometimes, they also burnt the forest in which they thought animals will be and those Tangpangs will be waiting for the animal in front side.[58]

Sometimes, a group of people will go out for hunting far away from their village and stayed for some days said around one week for hunting animals. When they were successful, they will return back to their village. There are also cases in which they were unsuccessful. When they were successful and killed wild animals like tiger, lion, bear and other wild animals, before entering their village, to let it know the villagers that they were successful, they shot guns according to the number of animals they killed. When the villagers heard it, both women and children will run out with rice beer to welcome them. In such way, they entered their village happily.

Gamsa Hawmdan (distribution of parts of animals killed)

Customarily, when the early Thangkhals hunted down animals, they distributed almost all the meats to their kith and kins. They distributed the meats in the following manners:

a) *Upa sa* (Head and inner portion): The head and all the inner portion (liver, lung, intestine) of the animal are considered as Upa Sa which means meat of the elder and was given to the eldest brother of the family that is of the clan.

b) *Sa ngawng* (Neck portion): This portion was given to the maternal grandfather or eldest maternal uncle.

c) A *awmphel Langkhat* (half of the chest): This portion was given to his father-in-law or if he was not there to the eldest maternal brother-in-law if he is a married one.

d) A *awmphel lehlam* (another half of the chest): Another half of the chest portion was given to Zawl which was a close and dear friend.

e) A *liang langkhat* (one of the forelegs): One of the fore legs was given to the village chief as it was a meat due to the chief.

f) *Sakhuailu*: A part of the meat extracted from the upper portion of the thigh from the hind leg, given to the Manchilli.

g) A portion of the meat was given to *Samulman pa*, which means the one who reached to the place where the animal was killed or to the one who killed the animal if the animal did not died at the first shot.

h) The rest of the meat would be distributed to every household of the village.[59]

i) One of the thigh was given to the gun owner as gun's fee.[60]

Thus, the early Thangkhals had distributed almost all the meats of the animal they killed leaving very few share for themselves when they killed an animal.

Sangawng

Sangawng in Thangkhal means the neck of an animal. According to the customary law of the Thangkhals, if a person is in a position to kill an animal whether a domestic or wild animal, he has to give the neck portion to his maternal grandfather or if he is not there, to the eldest maternal uncle or if he was not there, to the eldest son of the maternal uncle.[61] It is customary to give it and by giving, it shows the love tied between them as well as a sign of respect to them. If they did not give them, he can be fine with sialpi (mithun).Thus, it is compulsory for a man to give the neck portion of the animal he killed to his maternal grandfather or to maternal uncle.

Salu (Animal's Head)

According to the customary law of the Thangkhals, if the younger brother were in a position to kill any animal, he has to give the head of the animal to his eldest brother. Here eldest brother means the eldest man of the clan and not necessarily his own brother. The eldest brother would put up the animal's head at the wall of his front house and maintain with pride as a souvenir. If anyone of the younger brothers did not give the animal's head, he was liable to be fine.[62]

Saliang

Saliang means the fore leg of an animal. According to the customary law of the Thangkhal, if anyone caught an animal, saliang was always given to the chief of the village. It was a meat due to the chief to every villager if they catch animal. Those who do not give this due to the chief, a fine will be imposed on them.

Thangkam dan (traps)[63]

Since time immemorial, the Thangkhals used to set up different kinds of traps to catch animals. Some of these are:

Sakhi Thang

Sakhi means deer. It was a trap made on the way of the animals in the jungle. Though the trap signifies the type of trap meant for catching deer, any animal that goes on that way were caught in this type of trap.

Lam Thang

Lam means way or road and *thang* means trap. Therefore, Lamthang means a trap set up to catch animal which go on the way. This trap is means not only for catching a particular animal but any animal that go on the way will be trap.

Pial

It is a trap made to catch animals in a place which are suitable for it. It is a trap in which on top of the trap - big log, stone or any other heavy things are kept in such a way that any animal that goes under it would be catch by falling down all those things which are kept on it. In such trap, big and small animals like bears, tiger, boar, etc. are caught

Thauthang

Thau means gun and thang means trap. Thus, as the name suggest, it was a trap lay to catch animal with gun. It was a kind of trap which would be fixed on the way in which the animal would come in such a way that any animal that passed by would let off the triggers and thereby shot that animal without missing it. In such trap, different kinds of animals are caught.

Melmuh

Melmuh means things which are taken by her eldest brother or eldest nephew (son of the married woman's brother). This Melmuh is given to the maternal uncle or son of the maternal uncle when their aunt died by the sons of their aunt. There is no fixed thing to be taken but it depends on the capabilities of their maternal nephew or cousin. But mostly a pot was given. This was done to remember their sister or aunt by her relatives and it was a must for the Thangkhals to do it.[64]

Teipi-Belpi

Tei-Belpi means spear and big pot. According to the Thangkhal Customary Law, the maternal nephew takes TEIPI-BELPI after the death of their last cousin brother (i.e. last surviving son of their aunt) from their nephew (son of their cousin). When their last cousin brother die, at the earliest convenience, the maternal uncle or nephew will bring a boar or pig and killed it in the house of their nephew or cousin brother and eat it together. In return, the sons of their cousin (grandsons of their aunt) will give TEIPI-BELPI to their maternal uncle or maternal cousin brother. Among the Thangkhals, taking of Teipi-Belpi after the death of their aunt's last surviving son is a must and is taken to make the family tied closer even after the death of their aunt.[65]

In a Mishi (death in once house)

Mishi means dead. If someone dies accidently where he or she is on journey or at any time in another's house, it is called In a Mishi. In such cases, it is necessary for his or her relatives to bring a pot of rice beer, a dog and a pig and killed both the animals and eat and drink together at the earliest convenience which is called *in sil* meaning cleaning the house.[66] This was customary for a Thangkhal to do this *in sil* when someone died in one's house.

Phungkik (Returning back to parent's house)

A woman, after the death of her husband if returned back to her parents is called Phungkik in Thangkhal. In such cases, she cannot make any claim on the properties i.e. moveable or unmovable which they already had during the life time of her husband.[67] All their properties as well as their children if they had were to be look after by the eldest brother of her husband.

Ngohkhial

Ngohkhial is a Thangkhal word which means one who is supposed of doing thing if he or she is not. For example, if someone may blame any other person for something they lost or doing something which the person did not agreed, in such cases, they were brought together in the village court, presided over by the chief. The case will be decided by the village council and if any agreement cannot be reach, the court will decide that they will do *aisan*. For this, the village priest will make his chant and do the *aisan* i.e both the parties will send their representatives. Both the representatives were asked to enter into the water and the one who was wrong cannot stay inside the water. It was supposed that the one who cannot stay inside the water was considered to be wrong and they were asked to return what they have taken. The loser party were also fined *salam* (a pig with which the court arranged feast) for asking forgiveness. Besides, they were also fined a traditional shawl which was given to the winner party.[68] In this way, the early Thangkhals decided cases when there was any difficult situation arises in deciding any cases.

Tousa (Feast for the eldest brother)

Tousa is a feast given by a younger brother to the eldest brother. Tou means Lord and Sa means meat or feast.[69] Therefore, it means a feast given to their lord or their eldest brother. Among the Thangkhals, the law of primogeniture is practiced and as such the eldest brother became the inheriting brother. Every non inheriting brother after getting married and separated from the parental home has to offer Tousa to the household of the heir. Even if he cannot give during the life time of his inheriting brother, he can also even give to the son of the heir after the death of the heir. Ordinarily, pig is reared by the family of the non-inheriting brother for this Tousa.[70] The first pig reared by the non-inheriting brother after he separated from his parental house is used for this feast.

This feast is counted as a reflection of a wife's capability and efficiency. Every married brother after they separated from the parental (inheriting) home is expected to offer at least one Tousa to his eldest brother. However, there is no time bound for offering Tousa. It normally depends on the capability of the non-inheriting brother to do it. Poverty of the brother may also delay it but at least one feast is a minimal and is a must and who perform this feast is regarded as well-behaved man in the Thangkhal society.

It is believed that Tousa is an expression of gratitude to the eldest brother for all the cares and responsibilities taken by the eldest brother for his younger brothers. The younger brother is not supposed to be free from the control of his eldest brother before he gives at least one Tousa. Consequently, it is also said that the younger brother can move or migrate away from the eldest brother after giving him at least one Tousa.[71] Giving at least one Tousa to the eldest brother released the younger brother from the direct control of his eldest brother and to take any decision of his choice. Thus, in the Thangkhal society, giving Tousa to the eldest brother is a must and is a very important step in freeing the younger brother from the control of their eldest brother.

Mouzunek

This means drinking and eating of *zu* and meat to celebrate the marriage of a girl at least once in their life time. This was done by the girl's parents in the name of their daughter. On this occasion, one and all dear relatives from different places were invited, take *zu* (rice beer) till one got drank and fighting was a necessary evil.[72] This was one of the happiest and most memorable times in the life of the bride.

Ki-ak-gual-khen

When a couple agreed between them to divorce without paying all the arears of the marriage price or returning back all the paid marriage price or divorcing price is called Ki-ak-gual-khen in Thangkhal. This happened between the couples when the couples were no more in love with each other. However, this kind of divorce rarely happens among the Thangkhals.[73]

Upa Sa (meat for the eldest brother)

In the Thangkhal society, the eldest son, who is the heir of the father property has a privileges over the other brothers. His house is the principal household called Innpi[74] and he is the head of the group of the families of his brothers. Here, eldest brother does not necessarily means the eldest brother of their family but in reality, the eldest brother according to the Thangkhals means the eldest son of the clan or the lineage. He is also called *Tulpi Pa*. He had the privileges of getting the head, heart and lungs (most vital organs) of a game animal hunted by his brothers.

A brother may give the whole body of the animal hunted to the heir of his father's properties if they lived together in the same village if the animal is killed by the brother himself without having a companion in the hunt. The body of an animal killed in group hunting may be brought to the house of the eldest brother of the hunter who hit the animal first for division of the meat among the hunters. If by chance the meat is divided among the hunters elsewhere, the head, heart and lungs of the animal shall be brought to the eldest brother of the chief hunter[75] which is called Upa Sa. In return, the Tulpi pa (eldest brother) will than give rice beer to the hunters. The Tulpi Pa will hang a number of different skulls on the front wall of his house as a souvenir which shows that his brothers were skilful hunters. Even all the brothers who were in other villages also will give the Upa Sa to their eldest brother failing which they can be fined.

Pusa (meat for mother's brother)

According to the Thangkhal Customary Law, if a man killed an animal, he has to give the neck portion to his Pu i.e. father of his mother or eldest brother of his mother. It is compulsory for a man to give meat which is called Pusa to his Pu i.e. maternal grandfather or maternal uncle when he killed an animal. Non-payment of Pu-sa is a serious breach of customary law.[76] It has been liable to a fine of one mithun. As such, a man must give the neck portion to his Pu whenever he killed a wild or a domestic animal.[77]

Fine for Sialpi and Salam

Among the early Thangkhals, a fine of Sialpi and Salam was the highest form of punishment. This fine was given to the person whose crime was considered to be very serious. They have to fine Sialpi (one mithun) and Salam (a pig) in the court of the village council headed by the village chief when they decided the case. Some of the crimes considered by the early Thangkhals for a fine of Sialpi and Salam are as follow;

a) A man who divorce his wife,

b) A man who impregnate other woman,

c) A man who rape other woman,

d) A hunter who does not distribute his hunted animal to the villagers,

e) A person accusing another person of possessing evil spirits,

f) A hunter who does not give Saliang (chief's meat share) to the village Chief,

g) A man who elope with another man's wife.

h) A man who does not give the neck portion of the hunted animal to their maternal uncle.[78]

Fine for Salam (A fine of a pig):

According to the Thangkhal Customary Law, those crimes which are considered to be less serious are punished with Salam that is a fine of a pig. Here, Salam also includes a pot of rice beer. Some of the crimes which are punishable with salam are:

(a) A person cutting the village forest reserved,

(b) A person destroying or stealing others property,

(c) A person dirtying the village water source,

(d) A woman divorcing her husband.

(e) A person degrading or abusing another by his clan name.

(f) A murderer who does not perform a feast in the village.[79]

Guta (Theft)

Theft was not very common among the early Thangkhals. However, there were some people who usually committed theft in spite of its condemnation by the society. The punishment for a theft varied in accordance with the nature of the articles stolen.

Stealing can be in the form of clothes, paddy, cash, animals or any other things. When the theft was known, he was tried in the village court presided over by the chief. The person responsible for it was asked to return the things which he had stolen. Besides, the person was also fined salam (a pig) with which the village council arranged feast.[80]

Sialkhup *zu*

According to the Thangkhal customary law, the nephews (grandson) was to give an animal to their maternal grandfather or maternal uncle. In return, the maternal uncle or grandfather killed an animal. This is called Sialkhumzu. When sialkhumzu was done, the following rules are followed for drinking *zu*. These are:

1. Bangkhua from both the parties will compete each other;
2. Both Bangkua thuap will compete;
3. Both eldest daughters will compete;
4. Both second eldest daughters will compete;
5. Both Thusa from each side will compete;
6. Both the Zawls will compete each other.[81]

In this way, the early Thangkhals used to distribute cup of rice beer when Sialkhup *zu* was celebrated. In this drinking of *zu*, if one of the competing party first finish drinking the *zu*, he or she will give another cup of *zu* to his or her compatriot or competent which is called *zu* tulhbeh in Thangkhal. This sialkhup *zu* was done to make the relationship between the nephew and his maternal grandfather or uncles closer

Pu Zukholh

The early Thangkhals used to practice Pu Zukholh to show their loving kindness to their maternal grandparents or maternal uncles. When the nephew or grand children do Pu Zukholh, their maternal grandparents or maternal uncle will killed a cow or pig or a mithun according to their convenience. They also can give a cow or buffalo or a calf mithun in return. Besides, if the nephew or grandson dances, he will be given a cock.[82] This Pu Zukholh was also done to make the relationship between the nephew and his uncles more closer which was considered to be one of the most important things in the early Thangkhal society.

Death

The early Thangkhals, when they die use to keep the body for many days. The chiefs and the wealthy people used to keep the dead body for 9-15 days and those who are poor were kept for less than three days only.[83] When they die, the body was kept in coffin.

The early Thangkhals used to cut down big trees for making coffin when they die. From the big tree they cut down, they make hole to keep the dead body. After keeping the body, they closed and sealed with sticky rice mixed with water. Inside the coffin, the body will be full of water and the Tanus (son-in-laws) will insert hollowed bamboo through the stomach of the body. Fire would be kept up in the berth near the coffin. The body would thus be dried and the body liquid passing through bamboo pipes to the ground.[84]

In the traditional Thangkhal society, as soon as death took place in a family, generally it was the loud lamentations of the family which broke the news to the villagers. They also beat gong and bells to announce the news of the death. To let it know the news of the death to their relatives and friends in other places, they sent messengers known as sikou. The messengers never said that the person died but instead they said that he or she is seriously ill which shows that the person had died. The dead body was not disposed off until the relatives from other places arrived. All the villagers came to mourn over the death and gave condolence to the bereaved family. Besides, the whole villagers also observed the day as holiday and no one neither go for work nor go outside the village till the death body was disposed off.[85]

In the traditionl Thangkhal society, the young ones were encouraged to take active part in the funerals in order to comfort and share the sorrows of the bereaved family.[86] The young girls collected firewood and rice from each family for the bereaved family. Besides, some of the girls attended the young boys who dug the grave and gave water to drink. The grave was prepared somewhere at the outskirt of the village which is called Hanmual.

The Val-Upa of the village decided the site of the burial and the work was completed by the youths as per his instructions. The young men dug the grave. At the bottom of the grave, a narrow hole just large enough to hold the corpse was prepared. After the grave was prepared, the corpse was place at the bottom of the grave and was sealed with bamboo which was collected by some of the youths while the grave was dug.[87]

After this, the grave was filled with earth. Besides this type of burial, the Thangkhals also used another type of grave called Pangli a khuak which means a hole was dug out at the side wall of the grave which will accommodate the corpse. When this process was completed, the corpse was pushed into the hole and the main pit of the grave was filled with earth. This kind of pit was dug usually for the chiefs and their relatives as well as for famous persons of the village.[88]

When a Thangkhal died, it was customary for the Tanus to wrap the corpse with clothes. When it was to be carried for buried, the village elders tied the coffin with rope and carried in a stretcher by the Makpas (sons-in-law) to the grave. On the way, the relatives of the decease person weep or bow their head in sorrow. After they buried, they will come back to the house of the decease person.

The Thangkhals classified death into the following categories:

Saksi

A person who dies by an accidental fall from a tree or by drowning or attacked by an animal or killed as a consequence of some quarrel, etc. are called unnatural death or Saksi in Thangkhal. The Thangkhals regarded such death as a bad omen for the entire family and on this day, no one was allowed to work in the jhum land. The death body of such person is not entitled to get proper funeral rites as he would have received if he met a natural death.[89] The corpse was not allowed to remain in the village for the whole night and it was buried as soon as possible.

Naunei a si

It means death of a woman due to child birth. It was considered most unfortunate for woman to die in such condition. In such death, young women were not allow to go to the funeral as they feared that they might face the same fate if they go to the funeral and help the bereaved family.[90]

Sihpangai a si

It means a natural death. The death bodies of such persons are buried in the normal course and in accordance with the rules of the last rites. When a person dies in such case, messengers are sent to the near relatives and friends known as Sikou to inform them of the death. The death body will be buried only after their relatives and dear ones arrive.

Naupang si

It means death of a child. If a child dies in its infancy, such death is not considered as a normal death. In such case, the death body was not buried in the normal procedure of burial as in the case of a grown up person. The death child is buried in a pit dug beneath the floor of the house.[91]

The traditional death rites performed by the early Thangkhals was rather expensive. They have to drink *zu* together called Khunzu and killed four-legged animal called Kawsa sa. Among the Thangkhals, Khunzu means rice beer which was contributed for drinking when there was death in one's own house.

The following persons contributed khunzu:

a) Bangkua(head of the clan/family);
b) Bangkua thuap (close relative of the family);
c) Zawlpa (close and dear friend);
d) Nuphal (wife's sister or husband of wife's sister);
e) Sa khuailu sangpa (the one who got sakhuailu);
f) Sabeu Tangpa (The one who got sabeu);
g) Thusa mi nih (those who conduct the functions in the family; two men);
h) Ada thuap (the one who support the Bangkua); and
i) Aliang kung tawng tangpa (the one who got Aliang kung tawng).[92]

These people will contribute khunzu when someone died and it is also called Namsiat *zu*.

According to their customary law, Khunzu is a compulsory thing which they did it when they killed an animal after the death of a person which is called Kawsa sagoh. They will drink that rice beer which was contributed on this day. However, they did not just drink the rice beer but followed some rules for drinking it. The following rules are observed in drinking the *zu*:

1) *Tanu tak leh Bangkua kituak ding* meaning eldest daughter and Bangkua will compete in drinking;
2) *Tanu nihna leh Bangkua thuap kituak ding*; meaning Second daughter and Bangkua thuap will compete;
3) *Tanu thumna leh zawlpa ki tuak ding*; meaning Third daughter will compete with Zawl pa;
4) *Nuphal pa leh Pu ngong nepa ki tuak ding*; meaning brother-in-law (husband of wife sister) and maternal grandfather or maternal uncle who took the neck of the animal killed will compete in drinking *zu*.[93]

Besides, they will also call all the daughters from the bereaved family and they will get one share of meat and a cup of rice beer. Here Tanu does not mean only the daughters but also can mean their husbands. After distributing the *zu* to these people, the other people can start drinking the *zu* and they enjoyed it even though it was drink on account of death.

The early Thangkhals called the animal which they killed when somebody died as Khunsa or Namsiatsa. They did not eat up all the meat but also distributed some parts of the meat to the following persons:

a) Bangkuapa will get the thigh of the animal killed.
b) Bangkua thuap will get the fore leg on which they poured the *zu*.
c) Zawl will get the Khuailu of the animal killed.
d) The two Thusa will get the rib.
e) Nuphal will get the zaw of the animal.
f) Sasem will get the thigh meat.[94]

Besides, the Tanus present will get a share of meat and a cup of rice beer. All the parts of the meat which were left over were cooked and ate by the villagers.

In this way, the early Thangkhals have their own custom even in death funeral and in distributing the meat of the animal killed.

Sikou

According to the Thangkhal Customary Law, when a person died, to led it know all their relatives in other villages, they sent one or two persons to inform about the death of their relatives which is known as Sikou. Those Sikous did not directly tell that someone had died but they instead inform them that their relative was seriously ill. In such cases, they realized that their relatives had already died and immediately get ready and went to the place where the dead body of their relative was.[95] In this way, the early Thangkhals informed their relatives who were in other places when they die.

Taboos

The Thangkhals had different kinds of taboos to be observed by each and everyone. Some of these are;

1. In the Thangkhal society, Ki Saseng Leh meaning exchange by marriage was not permitted. For example if A (male) married B (female), the sister of A is not allowed to marry the brother of B. If they married against the wishes of the family, it is called Ki Saseng Leh. It was believed that in such marriage, one of the families would not get blessings especially the younger one and would suffer much hardship in life.
2. The Thangkhals did not permit members of a family to set out for a journey on the same day at different directions.It

was believed that either of the two would be unlucky to face any unforeseen things.

3. It was a taboo for a Thangkhal man to beat or kill any thing including insects or animals during the pregnancy of his wife. It was believed that his wife would give birth to a handicapped child if he did not refrain from doing all these.
4. It was a taboo for pregnant women to eat monkey's meat as it was believed that the baby which was to be born will resemble the monkey and will be very talkative. It was also forbidden for her to eat crab's meat as it was believed that her baby will be very slow and inactive and will have lots of saliva.
5. When a family had made some special sacrifice, they hang branches of tree upside down over their gates showing that they were having sacrifice. On such sacrifices, they cannot have guest and no one except the family members were allow to enter the house. It was a taboo to enter such house for others as it will spoil the sanctity of the sacrifice and they have to refund whatever was spent in the sacrifice if they happen to enter the house.
6. Cooking or frying a crab in the jungle was a taboo for a Thangkhal as it was believed that a lion or a tiger will come to help the crab if they hear the smell. So, no one is allowed to cook or fry crab in the jungle.

NOTES

1. Lewin, T.H.: *The Hill Tracts of Chittagong and the Dwellers Therein;* Tribal Research Institute, Aizawl, Mizoram; Reprint- 2004. p.142.
2. Mate, S. Haukhanlian: *Social and Religious Transformation among the Mizos (1872-1972)*; Ph.D. Thesis (Unpublished), Department of History, Manipur University, Canchipur, 2005, p.31.
3. *Paite in Mizoram*; Tribal Research Institute, Aizawl, Mizoram, 2011. p. 69. (Hereafter cited as Paite).
4. *Ibid.*

5. Lamkang, Sankhil Shethon; *The Social and Cultural life of the Lamkang Tribe*; M. Phil. Dissertation (unpublished), Department of Political Science, Manipur University, Canchipur, 1994, p.22.
6. Gangte, T.S.; *The Kukis of Manipur: A Historical Analysis*; Gyan Publishing House, New Delhi, 2003, p. 59.
7. *Ibid.* p. 79.
8. Ginzahang interviewed.
9. Niangdeihnuam; *The Study of the Thangkhal Tribe of Manipur*; M. Phil. Dissertation, (unpublished), Department of Political Science, Manipur University, Canchipur, 2008, p.77.
10. Gangte, T.S.: *op. cit.*, p.79.
11. Ray, Animesh: *Mizoram*; National Book Trust, India, Second Edition, 2002, p. 88.
12. Ruwndar, Kanthung: *The Social and Political Life of the Anal Tribe of Manipur*; M. Phil. Dissertation, Department of Political Science, Manipur University, Canchipur, 1995, p.39.
13. Chingzanian interviewed.
14. Niangdeihnuam; *op. cit.,* p.77.
15. Ginzahang interviewed.
16. Thangkhal Sinlai Pawlpi Souvenir, *Sinlai Suangphum* (1987-2008), p. 58. (Hereafter cited as Sinlai Suangphum).
17. Khupchinkhai interviewed.
18. Hminga, C.L.: *The Life and Witness of the Churches in Mizoram*; Published by The Literature Committee, Baptist Church of Mizoram, Serkawn, Mizoram, 1987, p. 31.
19. Niangdeihnuam; *op. cit.,* p.78.
20. *History of the Thangkhal People's Organisation* published by Thangkhal People's Organisation, 2003, p. 35.(Hereafter cited as Thangkhal People).
21. Niangdeihnuam; *op. cit.,* p.79.
22. Thangkhal People; *op. cit.,* p. 35.
23. Sinlai Suangphum,*op. cit.,* p. 59.
24. Kipgen, Mangkhosat; *Christianity and Mizo Culture*; published by The Mizo Theological Conference, Mizoram, 1996, p. 80.
25. Sinlai Suangphum; *op. cit.,* p.59.
26. Thangkhal People; *op. cit.,* p. 36.
27. Sinlai Suangphum; *op. cit.,* p.59.
28. Thangkhal People; *op. cit.,* p. 36.

29. *Ibid.*, p. 37.
30. *Ibid.*
31. Pudaite, Rochunga; *The Education of the Hmar People*; published by Indo-Burma Pioneer Mission; Sielmat, Manipur, 1963, p. 53.
32. Niangdeihnuam: *op. cit.,* p.80.
33. Shakespear, J.: *The Lushei Kuki Clans*; Tribal Research Institute, Aizawl, Mizoram, Reprint -1988, p.52.
34. Malsawma, H.L.: *Sociology of the Mizos*; Spectrum Publications, Guwahati, Assam, 2002, p. 30.
35. Rev. S.Khaisuanmang interviewed.
36. *The Zou Custom (Zou Tawndan)*; Revised and Corrected, Lamka, 1984, p. 5.(Hereafter cited as The Zou Custom).
37. *Ibid.*, p.4.
38. *Ibid.*, p.5.
39. *Ibid.*, p. 6.
40. *Ibid.*, p.7.
41. Ginzadal interviewed.
42. The Zou Custom, p. 6.
43. Thangkhal People; *op. cit.,* p. 37.
44. *Ibid.*, p. 38.
45. Khupzagou; *Zo Chronicle: A Documentary Study of History and Culture of the Kuki-Chin-Lushai Tribe*; Mittal Publicationd, New Delhi, 2008, p. 5.
46. Parry, N.E.; *The Lakhers*; Tribal Research Institute, Aizawl, Mizoram, Reprint 2009. p. 296.
47. The Zou Custom; *op. cit.,* p. 6.
48. Mccall, A.G.; *Lushai Chrysalis*; Tribal Research Institute, Aizawl, Mizoram,Reprint 2003, p. 114.
49. Lewin, T.H.; *Wild Races of South Eastern India*; T ribal Research Institute, Aizawl, Mizoram, Reprint 1978, p. 133.
50. Ginzadal interviewed.
51. The Zou Custom; *op. cit.,* p.9.
52. Thangkhal People; *op. cit.,* p.25.
53. Rev. Khaisuanmang interviewed.
54. Kampau Mate interviewed.
55. Gangte, Priyadarshni.M. (ed.): *Why we must be Mizo?*; Spectrum Publications, Guwahati, Assam, 2006, p.22.

56. Gangte, T.S; *op. cit.,* p.102.
57. Thangkhal People; *op. cit.,* p. 25.
58. *Ibid.*, p. 22.
59. *Ibid.*
60. Ginkhokam interviewed.
61. Thangchinsuan interviewed.
62. Thangkhal People; *op. cit.,* p.23.
63. *Ibid.*, p.24.
64. Kampau Mate interviewed.
65. Kampau Mate.
66. The Zou Custom; *op. cit.,* p.9.
67. *Ibid.*, p. 7.
68. Thangkhal Peopla; *op. cit.*, p.26.
69. Kamkhenthang, H.: *The Paite: A Transborder Tribe of India and Burma*; Mittal Publications, Delhi, India, 1988, p. 150.
70. *Ibid.*
71. *Ibid.*, p. 153.
72. Gougin,T.: *The Discovery of Zoland*; Zomi Press, Churachandpur, Manipur, 1980,p. 3.
73. Kampau Mate interviewed.
74. Kamkhenthang,H.: Op.cit.p.146.
75. *Ibid.*, p. 147.
76. *Ibid.*, p.170.
77. Thangkhal People, *op. cit.,* p. 23.
78. Thangkhanlam as quoted by Niangdeihnuam in '*The Study of the Thangkhal tribe of Manipur'*, p. 89.
79. Niangdeihnuam, *op. cit.,* p.89.
80. *Ibid.*
81. Thangkhal People, *op. cit.*, p. 48.
82. Sinlai Suangphum, *op. cit.*, p. 105.
83. Thangkhal people; *op. cit.,* p. 26.
84. Lalnithanga, P.; *Emergence of Mizoram*; Lengchhawn Press, Aizawl, Mizoram, Third Edition 2010, p. 19.
85. Rualkhumzo, *op. cit.,* p. 147.
86. *Ibid.*, p. 149.

87. *Ibid.*
88. *Ibid.*, p. 150.
89. Gangte,T.S.: *op. cit.,* p.112.
90. Rualkhumzo, *op. cit.,* p. 152.
91. Gangte,T.S., *op. cit.,* 111
92. Thangkhal People, *op. cit.*, p. 27.
93. *Ibid.*, p. 28.
94. *Ibid.*
95. *Ibid.*, p. 26.

CHAPTER 5

Conclusion

The Thangkhals are one of the many tribes presently spreading across the Indo-Burma border and as far as the Chittagong Hill Tracks in Bangladesh. They belong to the Mongoloid stock of the Kuki-Chin Mizo ethnic groups, speaking the Tibeto-Burman languages. According to their verbal tradition, the Thangkhals came out of Khul meaning cave, a place which has not been ascertained to any degree of certainty as their traditional home.

The traditional home of the Thangkhals is definitely not known but somewhere between Kansu in south China and Burma (Myanmar) is believed to be their earliest known home as these regions are considered to be the original homes of the tribal people. From these places, the tribal people including the Thangkhals started their migration, some moving towards Tibet, some towards Nepal and some towards Burma. As there was peace in Burma, they started moving in different directions and the Thangkhal group moves towards the south and lived in the Chin Hills mostly with what we called now as the Suktes. Till this period, no tribal group has their own identity as it is now.

The first known settlement of the Thangkhals in the Chin Hills was Ciimnuai. From Ciimnuai, they migrated to Taitaam and then to Mualbem. From Mualbem, they once again migrated and founded a new village called Thangkhal. The people in this village have developed a distinct culture, tradition and dialect which are quite different from their cognate tribe of Kuki-Chin-Mizo ethnic groups. As such, taking the name of the village, the people called themselves 'Thangkhal'. Today, the Thangkhals are found mostly in Manipur state especially in Churachandpur district and some scattered outside Manipur.

In the administrative sphere, the Thangkhals had evolved and maintained a system of their own which had slightly different from other tribal groups of the North East. The administrative system was headed by the chief whose post was hereditary. He was succeeded by his eldest son who is known as 'Upa.' In theory, the chief was the absolute within his chieftaindom but in practice he had to govern the people according to the customary laws.

The village administration was carried out by the council of ministers which was called Khosung Upas headed by the chief. The main duties of the Khosung Upas were to help the chief in his day to day administration. Besides them, there were the village priest, the blacksmith and the crier who were important persons in the village who helped the chief in the smooth running of his administration. The Youth commander who guided and give training to the village youths also occupied an important place in the administrative set up of the Thangkhal village. He was responsible for commanding the youths in times of tribal war and imparted strict disciplines.

The chief and his council of ministers enjoyed numerous powers and privileges in the village. The chief was the head of the village in every sphere of life. Nothing can be done in the village without the prior permission of the chief. The councilors were the first persons to be consulted in any decision making.

They along with the chief decided any decision to be taken in the village. They all were above the commoners in every work of life. They enjoyed lots of privileges like meat share, paddy share, free from compulsory labour and freedom to choose jhum lands before it was opened to the commoners. The village council also had the privileges of enjoying Salam which was a fine imposed on the guilty party when any case was decided which was a pig with which the council arranged feast. Though the chief with his council enjoyed lots of powers and privileges, they could not act outside the customary laws. However powerful, they too were bounded by the traditional customary laws.

From time immemorial, the Thangkhals had their own customary laws which dealt with their individual and social life. These customary laws served as the law of the land and everyone was bound to obey it. Even the chief and his councilors were not exceptions to it. Among the Thangkhals, the institution of marriage occupies an important place. It is the backbone of their society which brings the family relationship more closely. Marriage among them was a civil contract made at the consent of both parties concerned. They were not restricted to any particular clan or family. However, preference was given to cross cousin marriage that is marrying mother's brother's daughter called 'Neita'. The boy is expected to marry his Neita to bring the family relationship more closer. It also signifies the respect and deep rooted love for their uncles.

Bride price exists among the Thangkhals. Usually, it was fixed at five mithuns. However, it can be paid in easy installments. When a girl married, she takes some materials to her husband's house as dowry; some of which are compulsory while some depends upon the capability of the bride's parents. Though divorce was strongly condemned in the society, it occasionally occurred it. It can be initiated by either of the two but the initiator had to pay the fine for it.

Among the Thangkhals,the eldest son of the father inherits all the properties. The illegitimate sons had no claim over on it. However, if there is no legitimate son, they can made claim over it. The younger brothers have no share in the father's property. They have to move out of the father's house after they get married.

According to their customary law, if a man killed or traps an animal, he has to divide the meat to all the villagers after giving all the meat due which are to be given to different persons. Those who do not distribute the meat can be fine according to their customs.

Death usually occurs among the Thangkhals. There are different kinds of rites and rituals practiced in it. Death can be divided into different types according to the nature of the death. In some of the death, all the rites and rituals are performed but in some, all those things cannot be perform.

There are various fines and punishments among the Thangkhals. The severity of the fines and punishments depends upon the severity of the crimes they had committed. The most severe fine and punishment was sialpi and salam in which the offender was fined a mithun and a piglet. This was the most severe punishment according to their customary law. The crimes which are considered less serious were fined salam that is pig. Thus, to fine a person, it was determined by the nature of the crime.

Besides these customary laws, there are several customary laws which are practiced by the early Thangkhals. In most of the cases, their customary laws are concerned with the fines and punishments to be paid by the defaulters of the law. With these customary laws, the early Thangkhal chiefs can control their subjects and could lived peacefully.

But now a day, with the passes of time, many changes had taken places in the Thangkhal society. Many of the administrative system have been discarded. There is no more village priest, blacksmith and crier though the chief and his Upas were still there. But the chief and his Upas no more enjoyed much power as they enjoyed in the earlier period. In connection with their customary laws, many of the practices are discarded and have become things of the past. However, some of the practices like marriage prices, fines and punishments, naming of a child and many other customary laws are still practiced and preserved.

Glossary

1.	Angkawm.	: Adultery
2.	Buluh	: Going to one's house for fighting.
3.	Gam	: Village land.
4.	Gouluah	: Inheritance.
5.	Hanmual	: Cemetery.
6.	Hausa	: Chief.
7.	Hausa Upa	: Village Chief and His Councillors.
8.	Hei	: Axe.
9.	Inlam zonsa	: A feast arranged by the girl's parents when she got married.
10.	Inpi sap	: Court fee.
11.	Intuan	: Separated from the main/ father's house.
12.	Khuamual	: Outskirt of the village.
13.	Kikhen	: Divorce.
14.	Kiteng	: Marry.
15.	Lawmkai	: A group of young men and women

			working together in jhum fields by turn.
16.	Loulut	:	Making sacrifice at the field to please the evil spirits.
17.	Manchili	:	First cabinet member of the Thangkhal chief.
18.	Mei	:	Concubine or secondary wife.
19.	Meisia	:	Practicing polygamy.
20.	Mouvan ken	:	Dowry.
21.	Neita	:	Daughter of maternal uncle or daughter of mother's brother.
22.	Nam	:	A strap made of cane meant for carrying seu.
23.	Numei man	:	Bride price.
24.	Numei sual	:	Rape.
25.	Palai	:	Mediator.
26.	Pasian	:	God.
27.	Phiau	:	sickle
28.	Puandum	:	A traditional shawl.
29.	Pumhai	:	A paddy due given to the blachsmith by those who attached to him.
30.	Pusa	:	Household god.
31.	Pusum	:	A certain amount of money given to the maternal grandfather or uncle of the bride by the groom on marriage.
32.	Pu	:	Maternal grandfather or uncle.
33.	Sakhi	:	Deer.

34.	Sakhuailu	:	The solid flesh of an animal.
35.	Saksi	:	Unnatural death.
36.	Saliang	:	Fore leg of an animal.
37.	Salu	:	Head of an animal.
38.	Sangawng	:	Neck of an animal.
39.	Sannemla	:	Traditional song.
40.	Seu	:	A basket made of bamboo.
41.	Sial	:	Mithun.
42.	Sial khau sattan	:	Cutting of the mithun's rope.
43.	Sialpi leh Salam	:	A fine of a mithun and a pig
44.	Sialpi nuta	:	A mithun and her calf.
45.	Sialsunglut	:	Family ritual sacrifice
46.	Siampu	:	Priest.
47.	Sihna	:	Death.
48.	Sikkheng	:	Blacksmith.
49.	Som Haam	:	Bachelor's Dormitory.
50.	Sikou	:	Messenger sent for informing the relatives in other village when someone die.
51.	Sumtong	:	Place for grinding.
52.	Tangsam	:	Village crier.
53.	Tangseu	:	Paddy due to the chief.
54.	Tanu	:	Daughter.
55.	Tanupi	:	Eldest daughter or eldest son-in-law.
56.	Tem	:	Dao.
57.	Thangkam	:	Lying of traps.

58. Tousa : Feast for the eldest brother.
59. Tu : Hoe.
60. Tuilut : Immersion competition in water.
61. Zawlgai : Pre-marital pregnant.
62. Zawlta : Illegitimate child.
63. Zu : Rice beer.

APPENDIX I

MONTHS OF THE YEAR

THANGKHAL	ENGLISH
Gangpi	January
Phumkha	February
Doupi	March
Ningkha	April
Zingkha	May
Muakha	June
Seugawl	July
Khodou kha	August
Tawnkha	September
Vulkha	October
Kaukha	November
Thaman kha	December

APPENDIX II

DAYS OF THE WEEK

THANGKHAL	ENGLISH
Nipini	Sunday
Seppatni	Monday
Sepkitni (Sepkikni)	Tuesday
Nilaini	Wednesday
Ningani	Thursday
Sintawpni	Friday
Kiginni	Saturday

Bibliography

Published Works

1. Chambers, O.A : *Hand Book of the Lushai Country*, Tribal Research Institute, Aizawl, Mizoram, Reprint- 2005.
2. Chatterji, N : *The Earlier Mizo Society*; Tribal Research Institute, Aizawl, Mizoram, Second Reprint, 2008.
3. Gangte, Priyadarshni M: *Why must we be Mizo?*, Spectrum Publications, Guwahati, Assam, 2006.
4. Gangte, T.S: *The Kukis of Manipur: A Historical Analysis*; Gyan Publishing House, New Delhi, 2003.
5. Gougin, T: *Discovery of Zouland*; Churachndpur, 1980.
6. Hall, D.G.E: *A History of South East Asia*; MacMillan Co. Ltd., London, 1955.
7. *History of the Thangkhal People's Organisation* Published by Thangkhal People Organisation, Lamka, Manipur, 2003.
8. Hluna, J.V: *Education and Missionaries in Mizoram*; Spectrum Publications, Guwahati, Assam, 1992.
9. Hminga, C.L: *The life and Witness of the Churches in Mizoram*; Published by The Literature Committee, Baptist Church of Mizoram, Serkawn, Mizoram, 1987.

10. Khupzago : *Zo Chronicle: A Documentary Study of History and Culture of the Kuki-Chin-Lushai Tribe*; Mittal Publications, New Delhi, India, 2008.

11. Kipgen, Mangkhosat: *Christianity and Mizo Culture*; Published by The Mizo Theological Conference, Mizoram, 1996.

12. Lalnithanga, P: *Emergence of Mizoram*; Lengchhawn Press, Aizawl, Mizoram, 2010.

13. Lewin, T.H: *The Hill Tracts of Chittagong and the Dwellers Therein*; Tribal Research Institute, Aizawl, Mizoram, Reprint-2004.

14. Lewin, T.H: *Wild Races of South Eastern India*; Tribal Research Institute, Aizawl, Mizoram, Reprint- 1978.

15. Mackenzie, Alexander: *The North-East Frontier of India*; Mittal Publications, New Delhi, India, Reproduced-2007.

16. Malsawma, H.L: *Sociology of the Mizos*; Spectrum Publications, Guwahati, Assam, 2002.

17. McCall, A.G: *Lushai Chrysalis*; Tribal Research Institute, Aizawl, Mizoram, Reprint- 2003.

18. Nunthara, C: *Mizoram: Society and Polity*; Indus Publishing Company, New Delhi, 1996.

19. *Paite in Mizoram*; Tribal Research Institute, Mizoram, 2011.

20. Parry, N.E: *A Monograph of Lushai Customs and Ceremonies*; Tribal Research Institute, Aizawl, Mizoram, Reprint-1988.

21. Parry, N.E: *The Lakhers*, Tribal Research Institute, Aizawl, Mizoram, Reprint-2009.

22. Pudaite, Rochunga: *The Education of the Hmar People*; Indo-Burma Pioneer Mission, Sielmat, Manipur, 1963.

23. Ray, Animesh: *Mizoram*; National Book Trust, India, Second-2002.

24. Ralte, Benjamin & Malsawmliana, ed, : *Social, Economic and Political History of the Mizos*; EBH Publications, G, Guwahati, Assam, 2011.

25. Rao, V.Venkata: *A Century of Tribal Politics in north East India, 1874-2974*; S. Chand & Company Ltd., New Delhi, 1976.

26. Rao, V.Venkata, Gangte, T.S. & Devi, Ksh.Bimola: *A Century of Government and Politics in North East India, Vol. IV: Manipur*; S.Chand & Company Ltd., New Delhi, 1991.

27. Rao, V.Venkata, Thangsanga.H, Hazarika, Niru: *A Century of Government and Politics in North East India, Vol. III: Mizoram*; S. Chand & Company Ltd., New Delhi, 1987.

28. Sakhong, Lian H: In Search of Chin Identity; A study in Religion, Politics and Ethnic Identity in Burma, Nordic Institute, Second Print, 2000, pp. 1-2.

29. Sangkima, ed, : *A Modern History of Mizoram*; Spectrum Publications, Guwahati, Assam, 2004.

30. Sangkima: *Mizos: Society and Social Change*; Krishna Kumar Spectrum Publications, Guwahati, Assam, 1992.

31. Shakespear, J: *The Lushei-Kuki Clans*; Tribal Research Institute, Aizawl, Mizoram, Reprint-1988.

32. Singkhokhai: Zo People and their Culture; Published by Khampu Hatzaw, Churachandpur, Manipur, 1995.

33. Songate, L.Hranglien; Hmar Chanchin (Hmar History); Enlarged and published by Rev.T.Khuma Songate, Churachandpur, Manipur, 3rd Edition, 1996, p.13.

34. *The Zou Custom (Zou Tawndan)*; Revised and Corrected, Lamka, 1984.

35. Tuck, H.N. and Carey, Bertram S: *The Chin Hills Vol. I;* Tribal Research Institute, Aizawl, Mizoram, Reprint- 2008.

36. Vumkohau: *History of the Zoumi (Chin) Race*; Zougam Research Publications, Lamka, 1990.

Unpublished Thesis (Dissertations):

1. Chinminlian, T: *A Study of Christianity among the Thangkhal Community*; B.Th. Dissertation, Asian Baptist Bible College, Bible Hill, Rengkai, Churachandpur, Manipur, 2011.

2. Lamkang, Sankhil Shethon: *The Social and Cultural Life of the Lamkang Tribe;* M. Phil. Dissertation, Department of Political Science, Manipur University, Canchipur, 1994.

3. Mate, S. Haukhanlian: *Social and Religious Transformation among the Mizos (1892-1972)*, Ph.D.Thesis, Department of History, Manipur University, Canchipur, 2005.

4. Niangdeihnuam: *The Study of the Thangkhal Tribe of Manipur;* M.Phil. Dissertation, Department of History, Manipur University, Canchipur, 2008.

5. Ruolkhumzo: *Traditional Administrative System and Customary Laws of the Hmars of Manipur*; Ph.D. Thesis, Department of Political Science, Manipur University, Canchipur, 2004.

6. Ruwndar, Kanthung: *The Social and Political life of the Anal Tribe of Manipur*; M. Phil. Dissertation, Department of Political Science, Manipur University, Canchipur, 1995.

Magazines/Souvenirs

1. *Thangkhal Bible Church* (IFCA-I) Silver Jubilee Celebration, (1981-2006).

2. *Thangkhal Sinlai Pawlpi* Souvenir, Sinlai Suangphum (1987-2008).

3. *Tamdil*: Silver Jubilee Souvenir (1984-2009), Government Saitual College.

4. Souvenir: Mizoram College Teacher's Association Silver Jubilee (1978-2003), p.11.

Persons Interviewed:

1. *Thangchinsuan* of Tuibuang, 70 years on 2.5.2011.
2. *Rev.S.Khaisuanmang*, Kanan Veng, churachandpur, 53 years on 6.5, 2011.
3. *Upa S.Kampau* Mate of Tuibuang, 46 years on 4.5.2011.
4. *Upa Ginzahang* of S.Geltui, 81 years on 9.5.2011.
5. *Lunzahau* of S.Geltui, 84 years on 8.5.2011.
6. *Upa Thangchikhai* of Ngoiphai, 80 years on 19.12.2011.
7. *Khupchinkhai* of T. Khuangkhai on 30.10.2011
8. *Rev.Khamchinhang* of S.Munhoih, 71 years on 8.5.2011.
9. *Khamsuanpau* of S.Geltui, 75 years on 8.5.2011.
10. *Rev. Khupkhochin* of T.Khuangkhai, 74 years on 26.10.2011.
11. *Upa Ginzadal* of Lanva, Lamka, 77 years on 1.5.2011.
12. Chingzanian of Tuibuang, 72 years on 1.5.2011.
13. *Ginkhokam* of Tuibuang, 83 years on 1.5.2011.
14. *Henchinthang Zou* of Aizawl, 73 years on 29.6.2012.
15. S.Khaikhanthang of Tuibuang, 54 years on 1.5.2011.

Index

• • •